Inside:

AF631633

The famous warships

NAVAL ARCHIVES

Vol 4 • First Edition • Lublin 2017

ISBN: 978-83-65437-48-8

Editor-in-chief: Damian Majsak
Assistant editor: Kamil Stopiński
Translation/Proof-reading: Bogusław Solecki
e-mail: redakcja@kagero.pl
phone +4881 501-21-05
DTP: Kagero Studio, Łukasz Maj

Editorial board reserves the right to shorten texts and changing of titles and also is not responsible for author's opinions contained in texts. Non ordered materials will not be returned.

Publisher:
KAGERO Publishing
Akacjowa 100, Turka, os. Borek,
20-258 Lublin 62, Poland
www.kagero.pl, kagero@kagero.pl

Marketing:
Joanna Majsak marketing@kagero.pl

Sales: e-mail: oferta@kagero.pl,
phone/fax +4881 501-21-05

The Large Cruiser of 1910, J-Seydlitz

Gary Staff, Marsden Samuel

SMS *Seydlitz*, torpedo nets hung out. The ship in 1916 [3D visualisation, Marsden Samuel]

At the beginning of 1909 the General Navy Department requested the State Secretary to define the improvements required for the cruiser of 1910, the new building *J*. Financial constraints meant that practically the cruiser size could not be increased above that of the battleships, and therefore there was again a trade off between speed and battle capabilities on a limited displacement, at least on paper. A memorandum from the General Navy Department set out some guidelines: speed as for *G*; either 8~30.5 cm or 10~28 cm guns; no weakening of offensive power. Triple turrets were considered, however, 28 cm cannon seemed acceptable, at least for 1910.

In August 1909 the Reichstag reiterated there be no cost increases, and a third sister to *G* was therefore considered, but rejected.

Meanwhile, Tirpitz was applying commercial pressure to reduce costs and pressured Blohm & Voss for a discount. He was successful with armour manufacturers Krupp and Dillingen.

On January 27th 1910 the Kaiser approved the design for *Seydlitz*, at a slight cost increase over *Moltke*.

Armament

Seydlitz was armed with 10~28cm SK L/50 cannon of the same model as in *Moltke*. They were mounted in a Drh.L C/1910 mounting with an elevation of 13½ degrees and depression of -8 degrees, giving a range of 18,100 metres, and in 1916 the elevation of the guns was increased to 16 degrees, with a depressions of 5½ degrees, improving the range to 19,100 m. The munition was 87 armoured piercing shells per gun of the L/3.2 type. These shells were propelled at an initial muzzle velocity of 850 mps and weighed 302 kg. It could penetrate 280 mm of nickel steel armoured plate at a range of 10,000 m. The propellant was

Seydlitz at Blohm & Voss dockyard before completion

Seydlitz undergoing trials

Another view of *Seydlitz* on trials

Specifications	
Building Dockyard	Blohm & Voss
Contract	21st March 1910
Building number	209
Keel laying	4th February 1910
Launch	30th March 1912
Commissioned	22nd May 1913
Displacement	Designed – 24988 tonnes, Loaded – 28550 tones
Length	200.0 metres
Beam	28.5 metres
Draught	Construction – 9.09 metres, Loaded – 9.29 metres
Moulded Depth	13.88 metres
Performance	Designed – 63000 SHP, Maximum – 89738 SHP
Revolutions per minute	Maximum – 329
Speed	Designed – 26.5 knots, Maximum attained – 28.1 knots
Fuel	Construction – 1000 tonnes, Maximum – 3600 tonnes
Range	4200 nautical miles at 14 knots
Cost	44.685 million marks
Compartments	17
Double bottom (as % of length)	76
Crew	43 *offiziers*, 1025 men

A beautiful picture of *Seydlitz* taken 4 May 1913

105 kg of RP C/12, with a fore charge of 26 kg in a silk bag and a main charge of 79 kg of propellant in a brass cartridge case.

The medium calibre artillery was 12~15 cm SK L/45 pieces mounted in a MPL C/1906 mount. With an elevation of +20 degrees the maximum range was 13,500 metres, which was later increased to 16,800 m. Maximum rate of fire was six to eight shots per minute. The total munition outfit was 640 armoured piercing shells and 1,280 high explosive shells.

Initially 12~8.8 cm SK L/45 guns were fitted but as with previous classes they were removed and their apertures were welded closed. In 1915 two 8.8 cm Flak were fitted to the aft superstructure.

The torpedo armament was four underwater 50cm calibre tubes. There was a bow tube, two broadside tubes and a stern tube. A total of eleven G7 torpedoes were carried. These torpedoes weighed 1,365kg and had a warhead of 195 kg. The range was 9,300 m at 27 knots, and 4,000 m at 37 knots.

Armour

With *Seydlitz* the armour thickness was increased compared to her predecessors. The main belt was 100 mm aft, 300 mm in the citadel and 100 mm forward. The casemate armour was 150 mm with 35 mm rooves. The forward conning tower was 350 mm and the aft conning tower was 200 mm thick. The turrets had 250 mm thick vertical armour, and the rooves were 100/70 mm thick. The deck armour varied from 80 mm aft to 30 mm, with 50 mm sloping armour. The torpedo bulkhead was 50 mm in front of the barbettes, and 30 mm otherwise. The barbette armour was 230 mm, however, as with all British and German ships of the period this thickness was reduced where the barbette was shielded by the belt armour. The armour was Krupp Cemented and Nickel Steel.

Seydlitz at Kiel Week, 4 July 1913

Sea Keeping

The *Seydlitz* was a good sea ship, with gentle movements but like *Moltke* manoeuvred ponderously and whilst turning well was heavy. The smallest turning circle was 448 m at 18 knots speed. The metacentric height was 3.12 metres.

Machinery

In *Seydlitz* the number of boilers was increased to 27 Navy type Schulz Thorneycroft, giving steam at a pressure 235 psi or 16 atmospheres. There were five boiler rooms. From 1916 tar oil supplemental burners were fitted in time for service at the Skagerrak Battle.

There were two sets of Parsons turbines. The forward and aft engines rooms were each partitioned into three, with the high pressure turbines on the outer shafts in the forward wing rooms, and the low pressure turbines on the inner shafts in the larger aft engine room. The centre compartment of the forward engine room was used for auxiliary machinery. The shafts drove 4 propellers of 3.88m diameter.

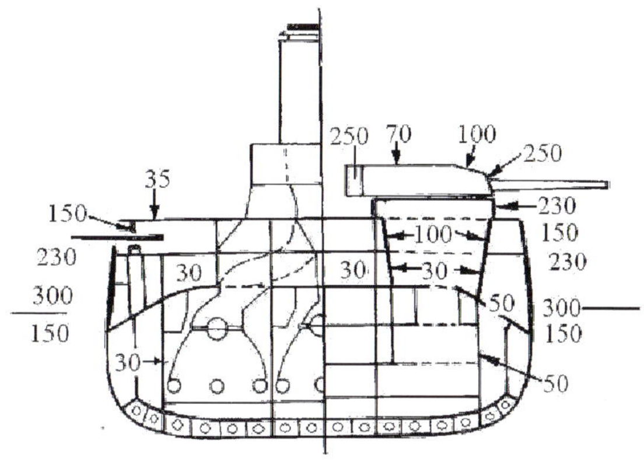

Disposition of armour for *Seydlitz*

Starboard view of SMS *Seydlitz* in 1913 [3D visualisation, Marsden Samuel]

Seydlitz at Wilhelmshaven after the Dogger Bank Battle

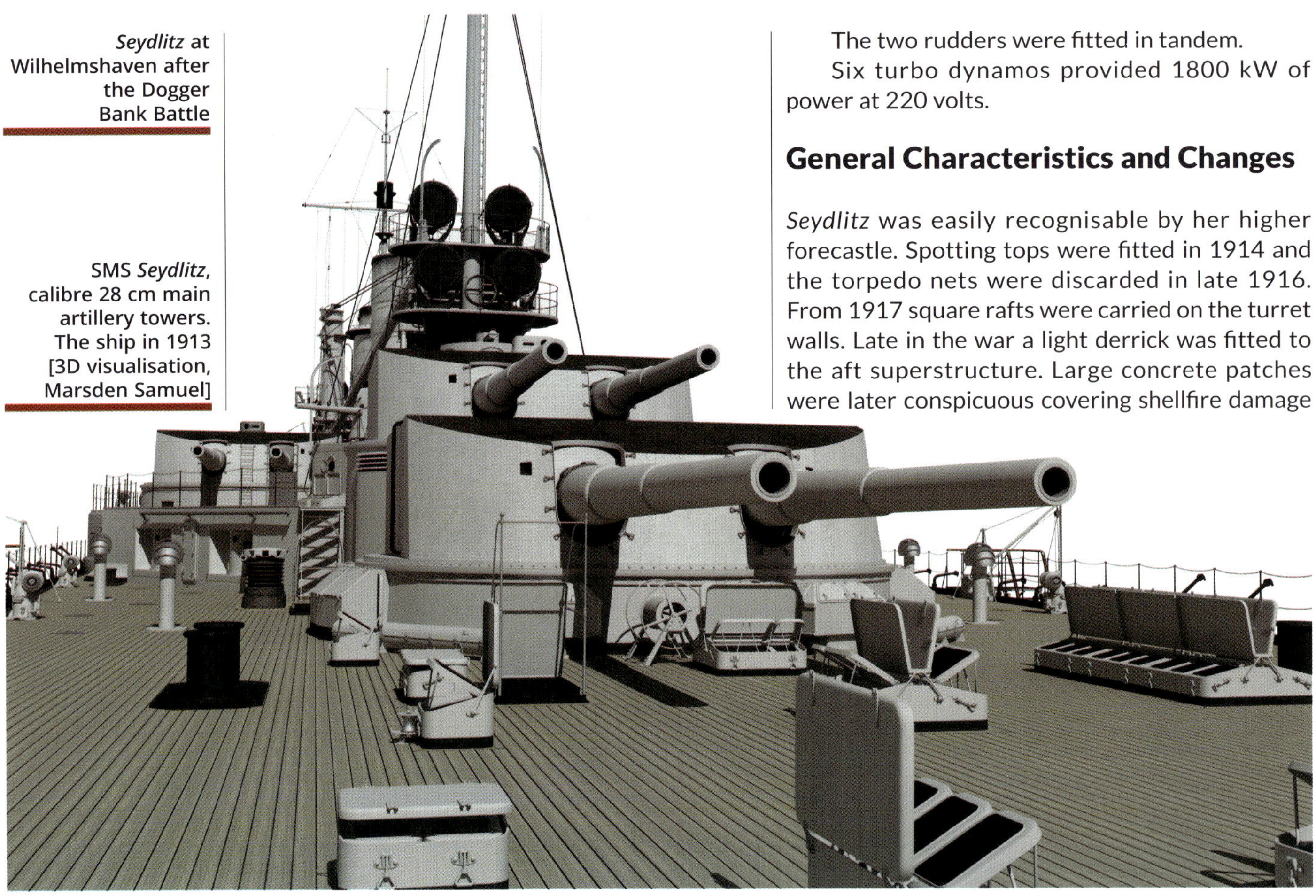

SMS *Seydlitz*, calibre 28 cm main artillery towers. The ship in 1913 [3D visualisation, Marsden Samuel]

The two rudders were fitted in tandem.

Six turbo dynamos provided 1800 kW of power at 220 volts.

General Characteristics and Changes

Seydlitz was easily recognisable by her higher forecastle. Spotting tops were fitted in 1914 and the torpedo nets were discarded in late 1916. From 1917 square rafts were carried on the turret walls. Late in the war a light derrick was fitted to the aft superstructure. Large concrete patches were later conspicuous covering shellfire damage

Damage to *Seydlitz* after the Skagerrak Battle

Two shell hits on the armour of *Seydlitz* during the Skagerrak Battle

View of amidships and captain's bridge rebuilt in 1915 [3D visualisation, Marsden Samuel]

on B turret and C barbette. After the aft group of 8.8 cm cannon were removed from the aft superstructure the structure was shortened.

Namesake

Friedrich Wilhelm Freiherr von Seydlitz-Kurzbach. *Kavallerie* General of Fredrick the Great, *Friedrich der Große.*

Service Record

Seydlitz was a further development of the *Moltke* at around 14 metres longer, but 1 metre narrower. She was launched by *General der Kavallerie* von Kleist on 30 March 1912. On 22 May 1913 she was commissioned with the crew from *Yorck* and following trials she joined the assembled High Sea Fleet near Helgoland and went on manoeuvres. On 23 June 1914 the

B turret of *Seydlitz* showing concrete repair patch after the Skagerrak Battle

Commanders	
Kapitän zur See Moritz von Egidy	5.13–10.17
Kapitän zur See Wilhelm Tägert	10.17
Kapitän zur See Moritz von Egidy	11.17
Kapitän zur See Wilhelm Tägert	11.17–12.18
Kapitänleutnant Brauer	Internment

BdA, Commander of Reconnaissance Forces, *Kontreadmiral* Hipper, transferred his flag from *Moltke* to *Seydlitz*, a position which she held, with brief interruptions, until 26 October 1917. She went on the interrupted cruise to Norway in July 1914.

Seydlitz led the Reconnaissance Forces in the coastal raid on Great Yarmouth on 2-4 November. On 20 November an advance was made north of Helgoland to integrate *Derfflinger* into the I AG.

On 15–16 December *Seydlitz* led the attack on Hartlepool. There was battle contact with four destroyers and *Seydlitz* was hit three times by coastal artillery. On the return journey the I AG was not supported by the High Sea Fleet and an opportunity was missed to join battle with an inferior part of the Grand Fleet.

The next operation took place on January 23-24th and resulted in the battle at Dogger Bank. During the battle *Seydlitz* expended around 390~28 cm projectiles and made many of the 24 hits made on the English ships. In return she was struck by just three shells. The first hit at 10.25 hrs struck the forecastle and did little damage. The last at 11.25 hrs struck the armoured belt amidships and likewise caused little damage. It was the second hit by a 13.5 inch at 10.43 hrs which caused severe damage. This shell struck the upper deck aft and then hit the barbette of D turret. The 230 mm thick armour was holed but the shell was kept out, however, a broken piece of armour and flash flame entered the barbette and ignited the fore and main charges found there. The flames went upwards to the turret and down to the magazine and ignited charges found there. The crew of the working chamber tried to escape to C turret and in so doing allowed the flash flames to enter there, and again the propellant charges were ignited. In total 6000 kg of powder burned in a few seconds. Only the resolute action by *Pumpenmeister* Wilhelm Heidkamp in flooding the magazines of C and D turrets averted disaster. The flames which engulfed these two turret flared mast high and caused the deaths of 165 men.

Seydlitz was repaired in the Imperial Dockyard at Wilhelmshaven from 25 January to 31 March 1915.

On 17–18 April, 21-22 April, 17–18 May and 29-30 May 1915 *Seydlitz* took part in fleet operations. From August 3rd to 21st the I AG, with *Seydlitz*, *Moltke* and *von der Tann*, took part in the Riga Gulf operation, forming a covering group. On 11–12 September the I AG covered a mining operation by the II AG to Terschelling Bank. On 23–24 October a further fleet advance followed. On November 24th *Seydlitz* was briefly aground in the Kaiser Wilhelm canal.

On December 4th whilst exiting the Kiel Canal *Seydlitz* ran over a net barrier and divers found it tangled in her starboard screws.

On 3–4 March 1916 the I AG participated in the first operation by the new Fleet Chief, Vizeadmiral Scheer—the reception of the auxiliary cruiser *Möwe*. A fleet advance into the Hoofden followed from March 5th to 7th.

View of Oldenburg towing Moltke on 25 April 1918, taken from *Seydlitz*

Seydlitz at a practice shoot

On 24 April 1916 *Seydlitz* set out on the operation to bombard Lowestoft, this time under *Kontreadmiral* Boedicker.[1] At 15.48 hrs *Seydlitz* received a mine hit, near the starboard broadside torpedo room. Just as with *Moltke*, although some torpedo heads were rent open they failed to detonate. A hole 90 square metres was rent in the side of the ship and a total of 1400 tonnes flooded into the ship. Twelve men perished. Despite the hit being outside the area protected by the torpedo bulkhead the flooding could be controlled and she was able to return to Wilhelmshaven under her own power at 15 knots. Repairs were completed on 22 May but a flooding test of the torpedo room on 23–24 May revealed more work was required so that *Seydlitz* was finally ready for service on 29 May.

A planned fleet advance had been postponed waiting for *Seydlitz* and she went into the Skagerrak Battle as tactical number 3.

Seydlitz had been hit 25 times by shells and by one torpedo and in return fired 376 heavy projectiles and made around 10 hits, the last 4 coming from 76 shots. During a night encounter with three English battleships she escaped by flashing their own recognition signal and turning away under cover of smoke. At around 03.40 hrs on June 1st she found Horns Reef when the deep lying forecastle scrapped over it. Because both gyro-compasses had failed the small cruiser *Pillau* was dispatched to pilot her home. By around 15.30hrs the situation became critical for the *Großer Kreuzer*, she was badly down by the bow and the wind had reached strength 8. Only the buoyant broadside torpedo room was keeping her afloat and preparations were made to evacuate the wounded. However, soon after two pump steamers arrived and with the help of dockyard tugs the heavily damaged ship was brought safely home. On the morning of June 2nd the outer Jade river was reached, and the following day *Seydlitz* entered Entrance III of Wilhelmshaven Dock. At worst there had been 5308 tonnes of water in the ship.

Seydlitz was repaired in the Imperial Dockyard Wilhelmshaven from 15 June to 1 October 1916 and after individual training was again combat ready in November. Although she again served as flagship for Vizeadmiral Hipper until 26 October 1917, an office administration ship, *Niobe*, was placed at his disposal on 20 August 1916.

On 4–5 November *Seydlitz* went to Bovbjerg on the Danish coast, together with *Moltke*, the 2nd Division of Squadron I, the III Squadron including *Bayern*, and the IV AG to recover the stranded U-Bootes U20 and U30.

From 8 November 1916 until 19 November Seydlitz undertook training in the Baltic.

On 11 January 1917 there were fleet exercises in the Helgoland Bight, which were repeated on 5 March. On 25 March *Seydlitz* entered the floating dock for repairs which continued until 28 March. The following day she went to Kiel and

SMS Seydlitz

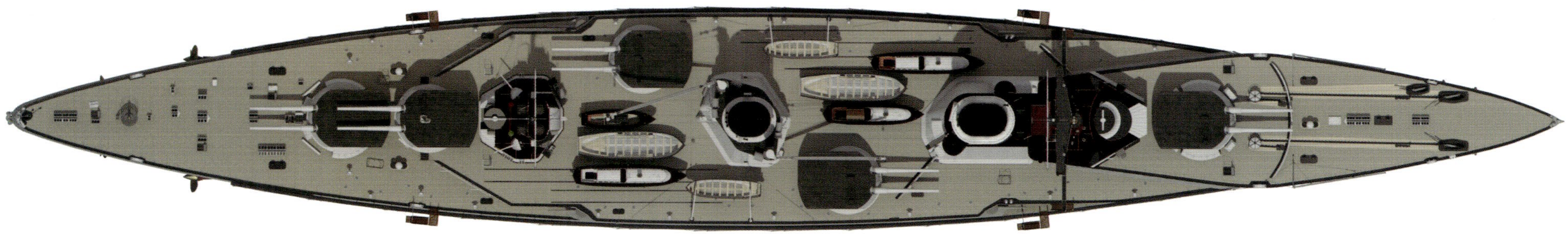

Drawings:
Marsden Samuel

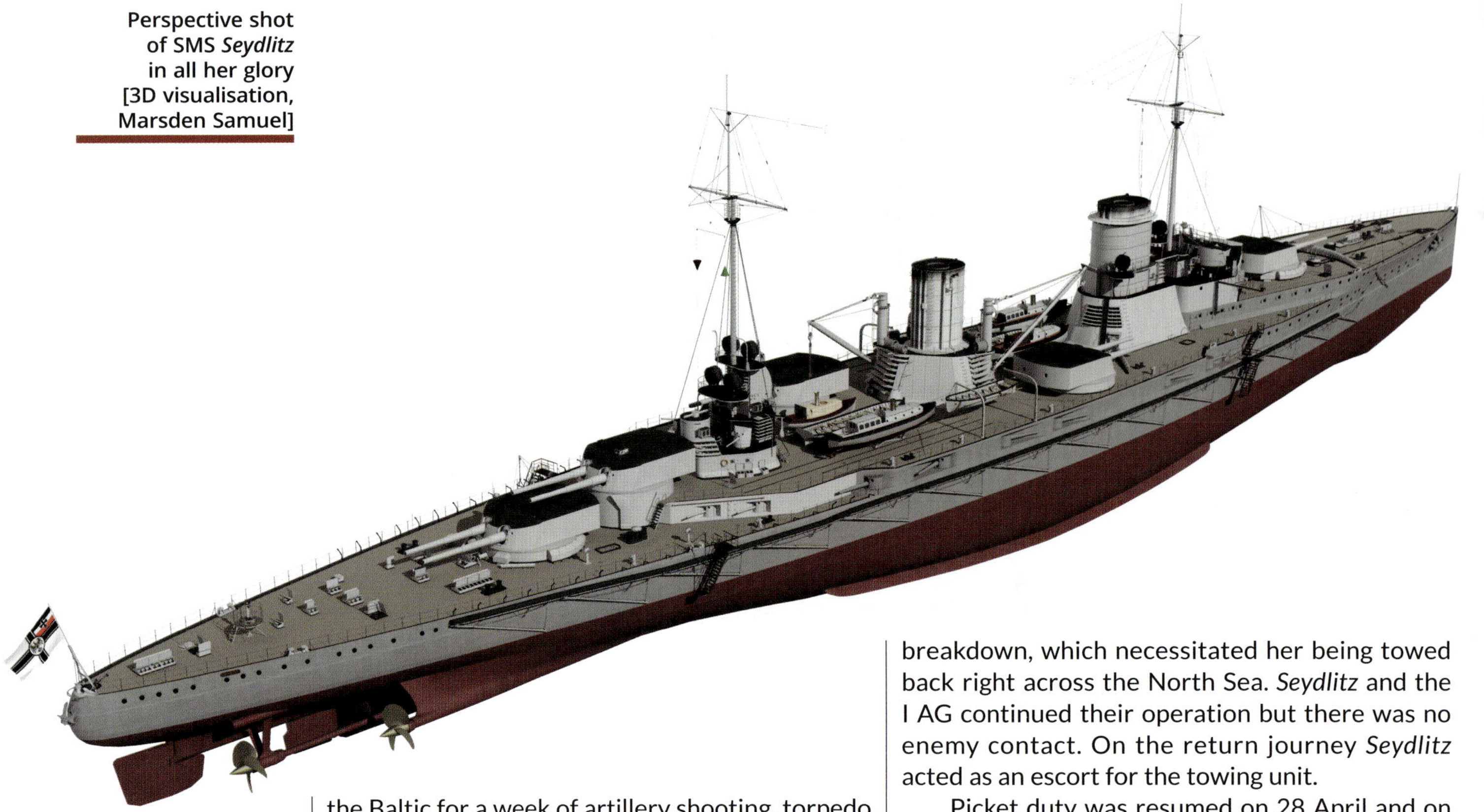

Perspective shot of SMS *Seydlitz* in all her glory [3D visualisation, Marsden Samuel]

the Baltic for a week of artillery shooting, torpedo shooting and tactical training, before returning to the North Sea on 7 April. Periods of picket duty followed and then fleet training exercises on 16 May 1917.

Another period of training in the Baltic followed from 5 to 23 July, before more North Sea picket duty, interrupted only by unit training on 19 August. On 7 October *Seydlitz* passed through the Kaiser Wilhelm Canal to the Baltic and from 9 to 11 October undertook training in the Mecklenburg Bight. The return to the North Sea only began on 13 November 1917. On 17 November 1917 *Seydlitz*, with Vizeadmiral Hipper aboard, ran out to support forces engaged against British battlecruisers in the Helgoland Bight, returning at 19.15 hrs that evening. There was no enemy contact.

From 7 to 9 December *Seydlitz* entered the floating dock to have her bottom painted before returning to picket duty.

The year 1918 began with normal picket duty and on 8 January unit training was undertaken in Helgoland Bight. During the course of 1918 *Seydlitz*, just as all the other units of the fleet, undertook regular operations into the North Sea to support and protect minesweeping forces. These operations took *Seydlitz* to the north of Horns Reef and to the west passed Terschelling.

On 23.4.1918 *Seydlitz* participated in the last advance by the High Sea Fleet to north of Stavanger in Norway. During the advance drifting mines were frequently encountered and that evening it was reported that the starboard condenser was salted. Repairs took two hours. Early on the morning of 24 April *Moltke* reported a mechanical breakdown, which necessitated her being towed back right across the North Sea. *Seydlitz* and the I AG continued their operation but there was no enemy contact. On the return journey *Seydlitz* acted as an escort for the towing unit.

Picket duty was resumed on 28 April and on 29 April *Seydlitz* supported minesweeping to the west. On 10 May the Panzerkreuzer supported a special minelaying operation, returning to the Jade the following day. Further support for minesweepers continued throughout May, June and July.

On 30 July *Seydlitz* put to sea as part of the I AG for an operation on Route 500, to punch a hole through the British minefields to allow a U-Boat to put to sea. The III Battle Squadron acted as further support. Many mines were encountered and the minesweeper *M6* was lost. The aircraft carrying small cruiser *Stuttgart* provided air support. *Seydlitz* anchored on Wilhelmshaven Roads early on 1 August.

Support operations for minesweepers continued and there were evolutions on 29 August and 23 September in the Helgoland Bight. On 23 October *Seydlitz* was docked in Wilhelmshaven for three days and on 29 October stood ready for the planned fleet operation, which, nevertheless was cancelled. On 31 October *Seydlitz* went into the floating dock for overhaul work.

Seydlitz was part of the fleet interned at Scapa Flow and was scuttled on June 21st 1919. She was raised in November 1928 and scrapped.

Seydlitz was one of the most popular and famous ships of the Imperial Navy, and was always know as a 'Happy Ship'. Her motto was 'Allen Voran"–'All ahead'.

IMAGES SOURCE: GARY STAFF, GERMAN BATTLECRUISERS OF WORLD WAR ONE, SEAFORTH PUBLISHING 2014

Endnotes

[1] Vizeadmiral Hipper had sciatica and was on leave.

KAGERO
Start
WW 1 & before
World War 2 & Modern Times
News
Modeller's Area
Download
Search...
Super Model
Wiosenne przebudzenie
Super Model best magazine for modelers
Super Model Magazyn Modelarski
THE BATTLESHIP ROMA 1942-1943
KAGA. THE JAPANESE AIRCRAFT CARRIER
The Japanese Aircraft Carrier Kaga - by Stefan Dramiński
Books returned from wholesalers
Zwroty z hurtowni
20% OFF
SHOP.KAGERO.PL
LICZBA SZTUK OGRANICZONA. KSIĄŻKI NIE ZAWIERAJĄ DODATKÓW.
THE NUMBER OF UNITS IS LIMITED. BOOKS WITHOUT ADDITIVES.
Kagero Miniatures
KAGERO MINIATURES
Kagero Miniatures CATALOG
HISTORIA BEZ CENZURY
SHIP CATALOG
KAGERO
avioner
NEWSLETTER
SIGN UP
Sign up for the newsletter to receive store information
CATALOGUE KAGERO 2015
KAGERO CATALOG
Shop online
Dornier Do 17/Do 215
Super Model INTERNATIONAL
HAWKER Typhoon Mk Ib
Figurine 1/24 Scale Mechanics
Super Model INTERNATIONAL SERIES
ARMIA
Błękitni strażnicy Niemiec
DOWNLOAD for FREE
Zmierzch Prowlera
portal armia24.pl
Aero
First
source
of information
www.kagero.eu

Hunt-class destroyer

ORP Kujawiak

ORP *Kujawiak* shortly after being taken over by the Polish Navy in 1941. The ship was painted dark gray all over. The tactical number L72 was painted on both sides and the stern

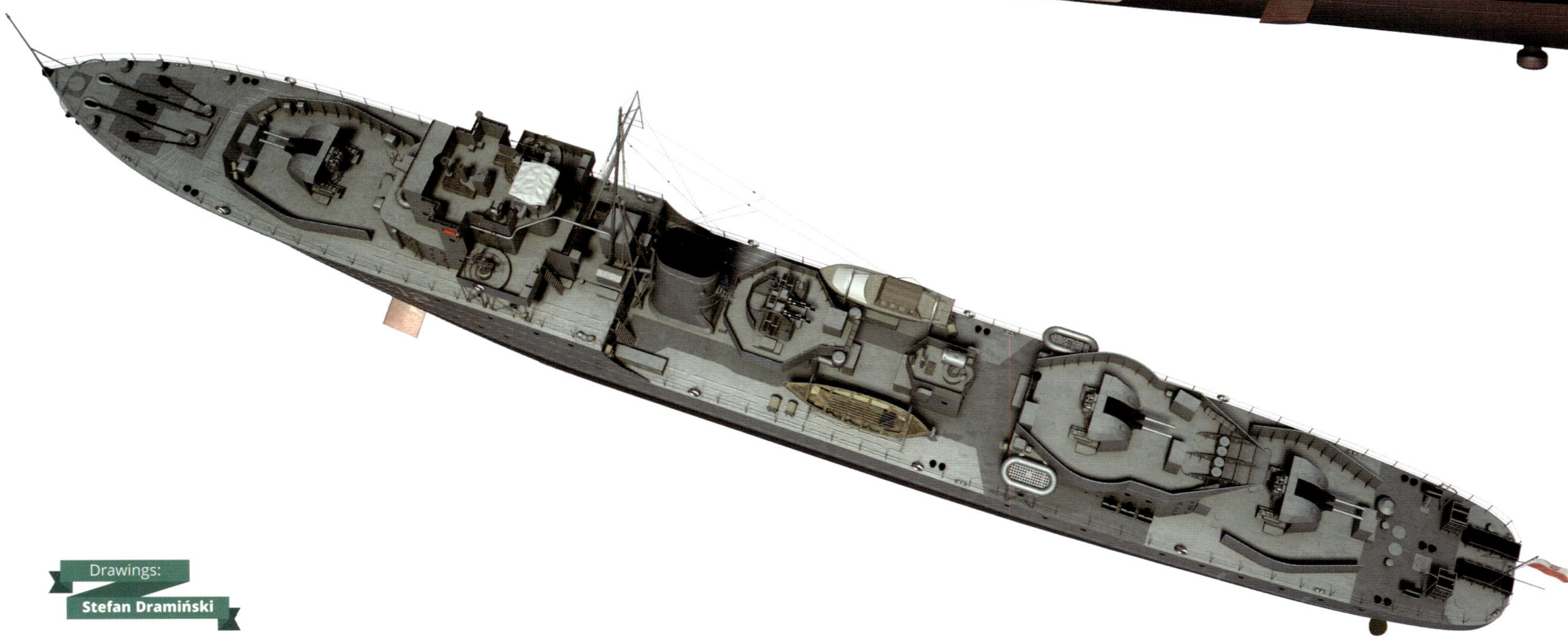

Drawings: **Stefan Dramiński**

ORP *Kujawiak* as she looked like on the day of sinking in 1942. The destroyer was painted gray, willow-green and dark dusty blue

Drawings: Stefan Dramiński

Hunt-class destroyer

ORP Krakowiak

The way *Krakowiak* was painted in 1943 when it was anchored in Algiers. It was light gray and dusty blue. During the repairs, the upper landing of the bow superstructure was enlarged, radars type 290 were added on the mast and radars type 285 were put on the range finder's roof, and additional stands for life rafts on both sides of the stern superstructure were fixed

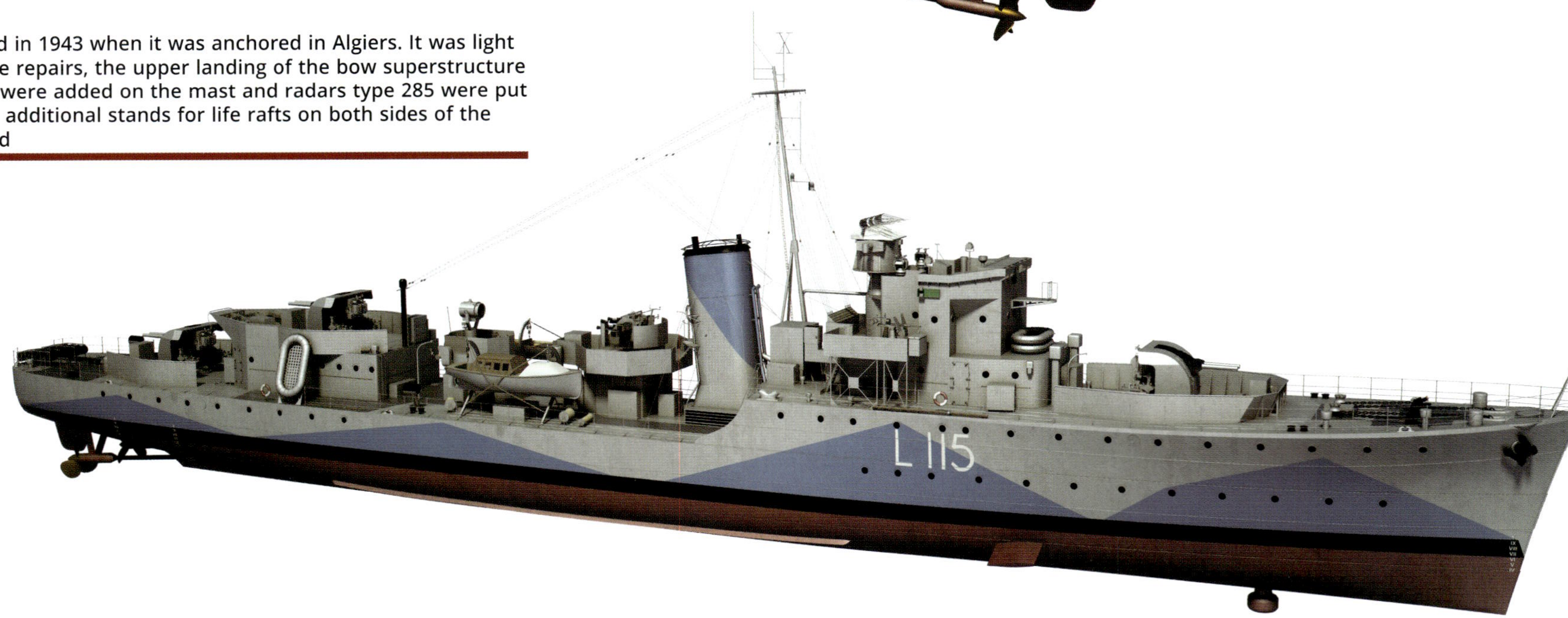

Drawings:
Stefan Dramiński

Krakowiak at the end of 1944. It was again painted in a simple way: the hull was light gray and willow-green, the superstructures were light gray and the deck was green

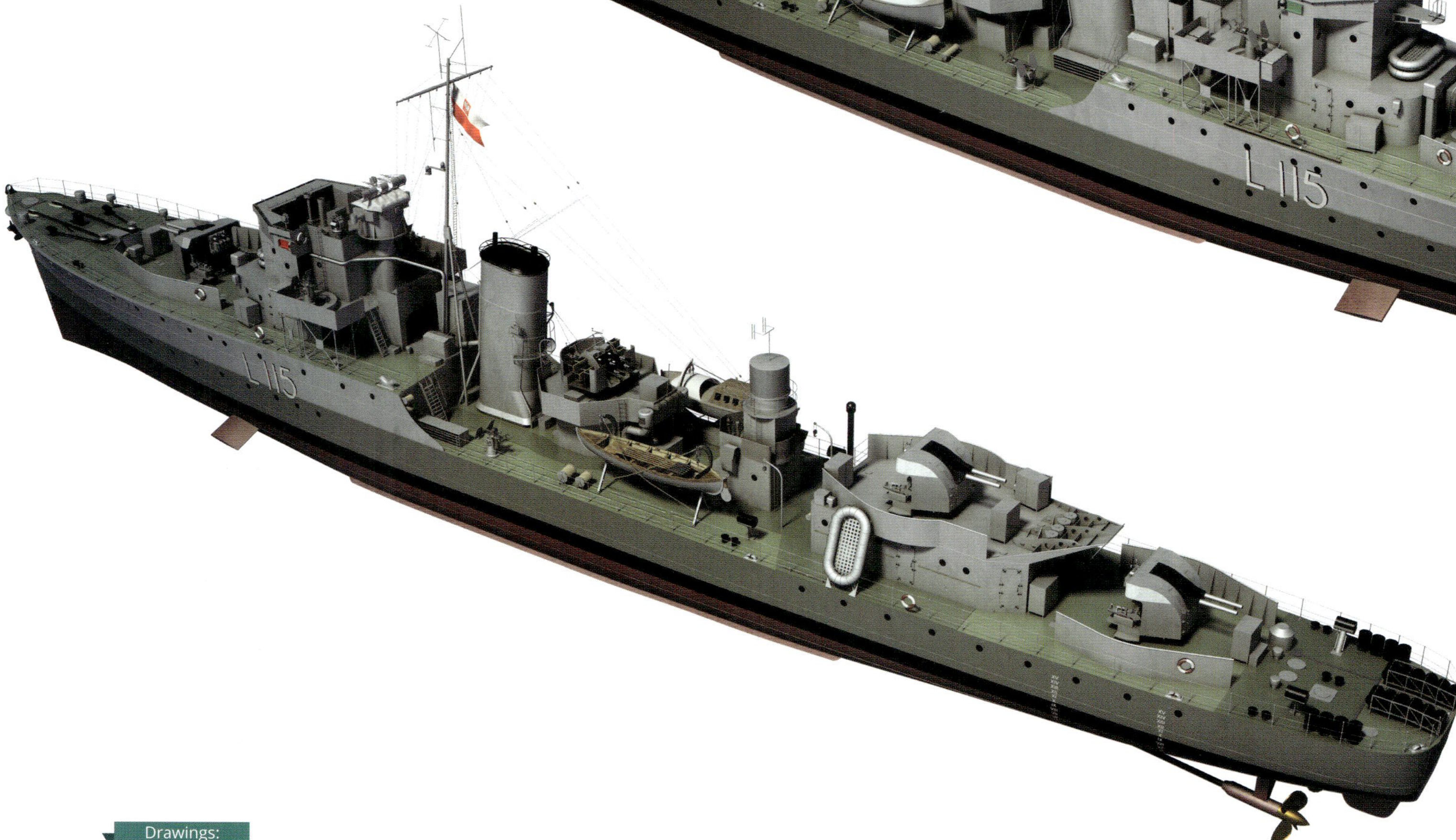

Drawings:
Stefan Dramiński

The Large Cruiser of 1911, K-Derfflinger

Gary Staff, Marsden Samuel

Quite correctly the *Derfflinger* class were considered to be the best battle cruisers completed up until the end of the First World War. Aesthetically they were also the most handsome. Design work was begun in October 1910 and continued until October 1912. Derfflinger had the sisterships *Lützow* and the near sister *Hindenburg*. The design represented the change to a new generation of German *Großen Kreuzer*.

After the final design of cruiser *J*, there were still outstanding issues for the following design. In April 1910 the General Navy Department was asked to prepare the requirements for the cruiser of 1911. The issues were primarily the number of shafts, machinery and armament. A three shaft arrangement would allow the employment of a diesel engine on the centre shaft. The advantages of this were better thermal efficiency, easier transfer of fuel, saving in personnel and the price. The General Department thought the change to 30.5cm calibre was essential. The weight increase of 8~30.5 cm guns over 10~28 cm guns was just 36 tonnes and the latest English battleships were fitted with 300 mm armour. If the cruisers were

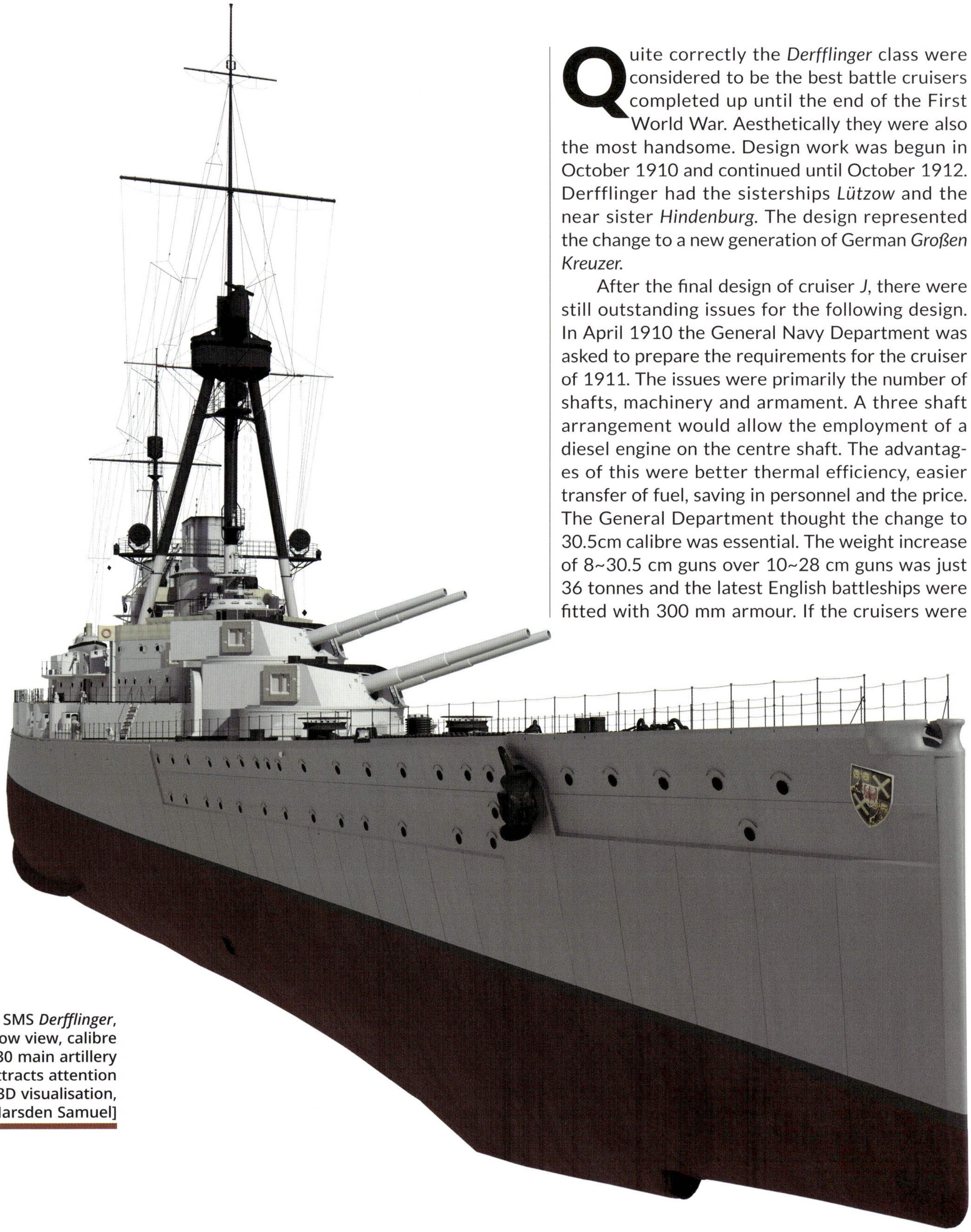

SMS *Derfflinger*, bow view, calibre 30 main artillery attracts attention [3D visualisation, Marsden Samuel]

Derfflinger shortly after completion

expected to fight in the line, the increase was mandatory. However, von Tirpitz disagreed and the matter remained unresolved.

Meanwhile *Geheim Oberbaurät* Veith determined that the large diesels were still not ready.

On September 1st a decision was taken for 8~30.5 cm cannon on the centreline. The armoured protection was to remain as with *Seydlitz*. In the interim the Kaiser had become concerned about the English "we want eight" program and desired the building time reduced from 3 years to 24 months. This was not feasible as the armour manufacturers could not keep up the production and neither could the armament manufacturer. This plan would also entail a change in the payment plan as the four yearly instalments would be reduced to three. The Reichstag would have to agree to this.

To save weight, a new type of construction was used that had hitherto been used on the Small Cruisers. The longitudinal frame system was used for construction of the lower ship's bottom. Previous large warships had been constructed with a system of mixed longitudinal and transverse frames. With an increase in the ship's length the demands on the longitudinal strength increased, and these demands could be met, with a lower weight, by employing a pure longitudinal frame method of construction.

The hull was to be partitioned in two, as with *von der Tann*, as this allowed coal to be stored inside the torpedo bulkhead. On June 8th 1910 oil boilers were mentioned for the first time. The advantages of oil were less weight, smaller boilers for the same performance, and saving in serving personnel. Steam could be raised rapidly and there was no tell tale smoke plume. The only major drawback was that the Navy would have to rely on foreign producers. Therefore, eight of the 22 coal boilers were replaced with 4 pure oil fired boilers.

Provision was made for the later fitment of Frahm anti-roll tanks. Nevertheless, the trial

A fine view of *Derfflinger* taken in 1915

Derfflinger with aft funnel painted red for an impending operation

A fine view of *Derfflinger* amidships, whilst at sea

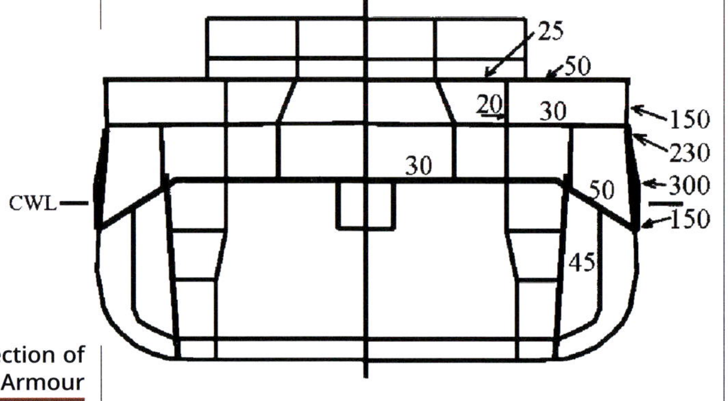

Cross Section of *Derfflinger's* Armour

Specifications	
Building Yard	Blohm & Voss Hamburg
Contract	1912
Building Number	213
Keel Laid	30th March 1912
Launched	12th July 1913
Commissioned	1st September 1914
Displacement	Designed 26600 Loaded 31200
Length	210 metres
Beam	29.0 metres
Draught	9.2 metres
Moulded Depth	14.75 metres
Performance	Designed 63000 Overload 76624
Revolutions	280
Speed	Designed 25.5kts Maximum 26.5kts[1]
Fuel	Normal 750t coal, 250t oil Maximum 3500coal, 1000 oil
Range	5600nm at 14kts
Cost	56 million marks
Compartments	16
Double Bottom	65%
Crew	44 offiziers 1068 men

cruise of *von der Tann* had revealed that the tanks only reduced the roll by 33%.

Armament

The main armament of this class was the 8~30.5 cm L/50 SK cannon. This gun could fire with a rate of 3 projectiles per minute, and the 405.5 kg shell was propelled at a muzzle velocity of 900 metres per second. The guns were fitted in the Drh.L C/1912 mount on *Derfflinger.* The turret was electrically trained and the guns were hydraulically elevated to a maximum of 13.5° before 1916, which gave a range of 180 hectometres, and after 1916 this was improved to 16.5° and 204 hectometres. As with the other cruisers the fore charge came in a silk bag, and the main charge was enclosed in a brass cartridge. A total of 720 30.5 cm shells were carried for a total of 90 per gun, 65 armour-piercing and 25 semi armour-piercing. With turrets A, B and C the magazines were below the shell rooms, on the lower platform deck, whilst with turret D this was reversed. Subsequently, *Derfflinger* was fitted with gyroscopic firing gear (A.G)

The medium calibre armament was the 15 cm SK L/45 cannon, in a MPL C/06.11 mount. *Derfflinger* carried 12 of these cannon as one per side was deleted to make space for the Frahm tanks. A shell outfit of 160 rounds per gun was carried, which initially could be ranged to 135hm, and latterly out to 168hm.

As built *Derfflinger* carried 8~8.8cm SK L/45 cannon, four in the forward superstructure and four mounted around turret C. Four 8.8cm Flak L/45 were mounted about the forward funnel. By 1916, the four guns in the forward superstructure

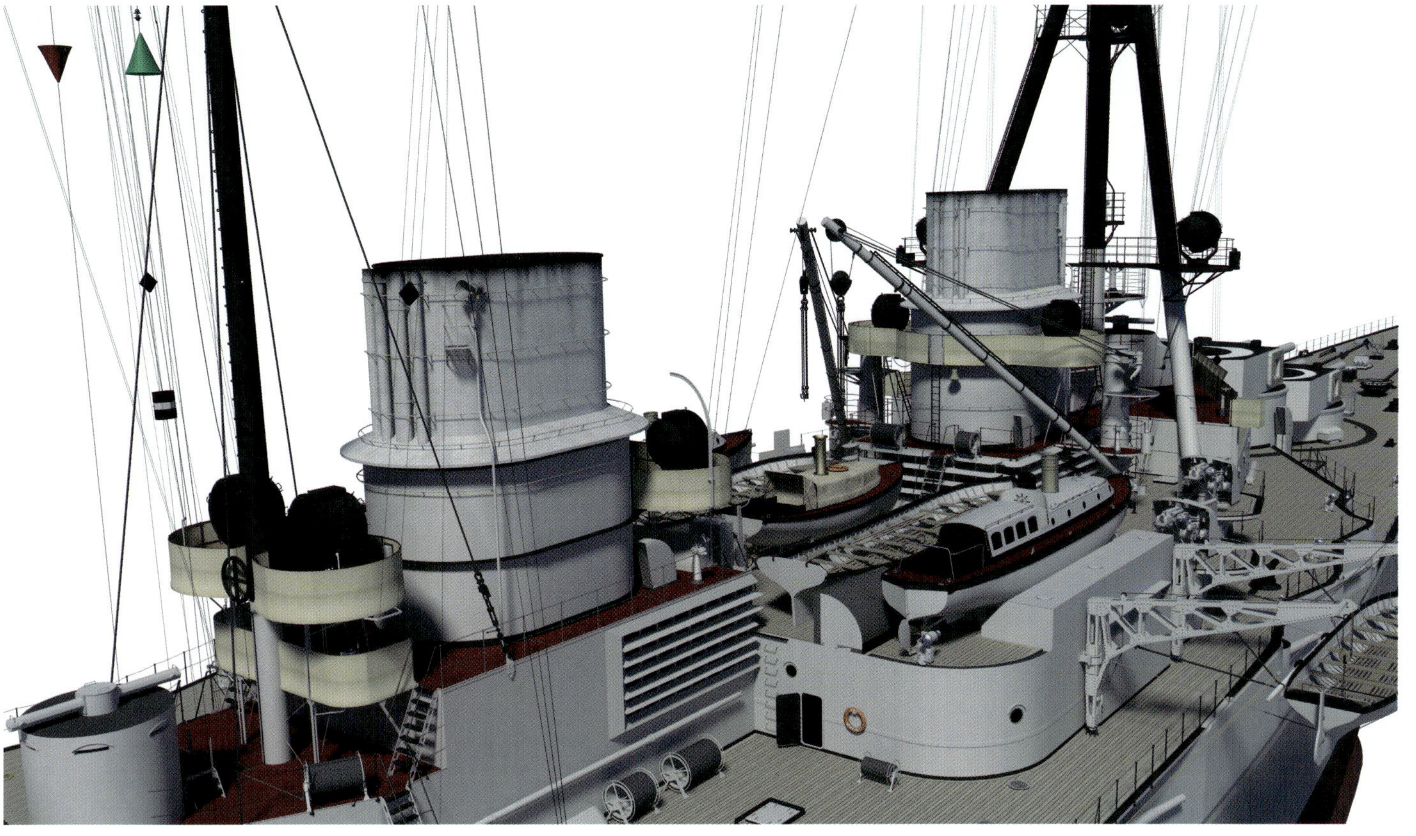

had been removed, and after the Skagerrak Battle the four aft 8.8 cm SK were removed. In 1918 the two forward most Flak were removed.

Derfflinger carried four 50 cm torpedo tubes and an outfit of twelve G7 torpedoes.

Armour

The armour of the *Derfflinger* class was similar in thickness to that of *Seydlitz*.

The main belt was 100 mm aft, 300 mm in the citadel and 120 mm forward. The casemate armour was 150 mm with 50 mm rooves. The forward conning tower was 350 mm and the aft conning tower was 200 mm thick. The turrets had 270 mm thick faces and rear walls, 220 mm thick walls, and the rooves were 110/80 mm thick. The barbettes were 260 mm. The deck armour varied from 80 mm aft to 30 mm, with 50 mm sloping armour. The torpedo bulkhead was 45 mm thick. The armour was Krupp Cemented and Nickel Steel.

Sea Keeping

Derfflinger was an excellent sea ship with pleasant motion. She manoeuvred well but slowly. *Derfflinger* turned well but was slow to answer the helm. The metacentric height was 2.6 metres, which was re-

SMS *Derfflinger*, amidships. steam life boats, searchlights and conning tower [3D visualisation Marsden Samuel]

Starboard view, the ship in 1917. Tripod mast attracts attention [3D visualisation, Marsden Samuel]

A beautiful picture of *Derfflinger* at sea in late 1918

duced from the previous class to reduce 'stiffness'. With hard over rudder there was a 65% speed loss and 11° heel. In a swell the casemates were reported as wet. The roll period was eleven seconds.

Machinery

The 6 boiler rooms were divided down the centre by a longitudinal bulkhead. There were 14 double, coal, Schulz Naval boilers working at 235 psi. They were provided with supplemental tar oil firing from 1916. The four double oil fired boilers occupied the forward two boiler rooms.

There were two sets of naval turbines. The forward engine rooms were adjacent to C turret and housed the high pressure turbines, working on the outer shafts. The turbo generators were installed on the deck above them. The aft engine rooms were between C and D turrets, giving the characteristic gap between these turrets. They contained the low pressure turbines, which worked the inner shafts, and condensers. The shafts drove 4 propellers of 3.9 m in diameter.

The two rudders were fitted in tandem.

The two turbo dynamos and two diesel dynamos provided 220 volts at 1660 kW in *Derfflinger*.

Derfflinger at anchor after the war

The diesel dynamos were located below the forward magazines, on the *Stauung*, or hold.

Derfflinger's machinery weighed a total of 3269 tonnes, whereas that of *Princess Royal* weighed 5019 tonnes. A further comparison of weights as a percentage of total displacement:

	Lion	*Queen Mary*	*Tiger*	*Lützow*
Armament	12.3	12.5	12.65	12.7
Machinery	20.2	20.2	20.7	14.2
Armour	24.2	24.5	25.9	35.5
Hull	36.5	36.1	34.3	30.5

General Characteristics and Changes

Derfflinger's funnels were of uneven height and had deep caps. *Derfflinger* was completed with a pole mast. After the Skagerrak Battle *Derfflinger* had a wide spread tripod mast fitted. There was a broad, white ring on top of each of the four turrets, as an aircraft recognition device.

Trials carrying seaplanes were carried out on *Derfflinger* in August 1915.

Namesake

Georg *Reichsfreiherr* von Derfflinger, born 10.3.1606, died 4.2.1695. *Generalfeldmarschall* and leader of Brandenburg *Kavallerie.*

Service Record—*Derfflinger*

The new building *K* was ready for launching on June 14th 1913 and was christened *Derfflinger*

Commanders	
Kapitän zur See von Reuter	9.14—9.15
Kapitän zur See Heimrich	9.15—4.16
Kapitän zur See Johannes Hartog	4.16—12.17
Fregattenkapitän/Kapitän zur See Von Schlick	12.17—11.18
Kapitän zur See Walter Hildebrand	11.18—12.18
Korvettenkapitän Pastuszyk	Internment

by the wife of General *der Kavallerie* August von Mackensen. However, after the hull had moved just 30-40cm it stuck fast and only on July 12th was the ship successfully launched. One of the wooden sledges had overheated and jammed.

Prior to the outbreak of war it had been planned for *Derfflinger* to be completed on 13 September and the Kaiser had ordered that the new *Panzerkreuzer*

Derfflinger after returning from the Skagerrak Battle

Derfflinger en-route to bombard Scarborough on 16 December 1914. *Derfflinger* follows *Seydlitz* and *Moltke*

SMS *Derfflinger*, starboard view of amidships. Calibre 15cm artillery, superstructure and tripod mast can clearly be seen [3D visualisation Marsden Samuel]

should be dispatched to the opening of the Panama Canal, which meant the cruiser would have to be in service on 1 October 1914. After that *Derfflinger* was intended to visit the 1915 Panama-Pacific International Exposition in San Francisco.

On 3 September 1914 *Derfflinger* transferred from Hamburg to Kiel. On 4 September she suffered damage to the port low pressure turbine, however continued trials. Then on 15 October there was damage to the starboard low pressure turbine. After repairs she was allocated to the I AG on 19 November 1914. A short advance followed on 20 November On December 15–16th she participated in the bombardment of Scarborough and Whitby.

During the Dogger Bank Battle *Derfflinger* inflicted much damage to *Lion* while suffering only one hit herself. A 13.5 inch burst on the 300 mm belt. Near misses caused some leakage and *Derfflinger* was again combat ready on 14 February.

Derfflinger took part in the Fleet advances of March, April and May, but on June 28th she suffered damage to the starboard low pressure turbine and was in dock until August.

Derfflinger pictured with two U-Boats, the near one being of the UBIII type

On 31 August *Derfflinger* returned to the North Sea and on 11–12.9 covered the minelaying operation to Swarte Bank. A Fleet advance followed on 23–24.10.

The year 1916 saw increased activity by the High Sea Fleet and under the new Fleet Chief, Vizeadmiral Scheer, an advance in the Hoofden was made 6–7 March, and on 25 March a counter thrust was carried out against English light forces. On 24–25 April a coastal bombardment of Lowestoft was conducted and a running battle with English light forces followed.

During the Skagerrak Battle *Derfflinger* was tactical number 2 and was struck by shells 21 times. *Derfflinger* was also hit by 2~6 inch shells and 7~4 inch shells. She suffered 157 dead and 26 wounded, the highest figures for a ship not sunken. She returned to harbour with over 3000 tonnes of water in the ship. The success of this cruiser during the battle led to the British sailors giving her the nickname "Iron Dog."

Provisional repairs were carried out at Wilhelmshaven and then she transferred to Howaldts Dockyard in Kiel, where she was under repair and modification until 15 October, which included the installation of her tripod mast. After individual training in the Baltic *Derfflinger* was combat ready in November.

On 21 November the cruiser arrived on Schillig Roads and began picket duty. Evolutions with the High Sea Fleet followed on 6 December. On 28 December *Derfflinger* ran out into the

A view of *Derfflinger's* forecastle

North Sea with *Moltke* before returning to Schillig Roads. Much of the normal North Sea routine followed; periods of picket duty, time anchored on Wilhelmshaven Roads and dockyard periods. There was Unit training in the Helgoland Bight on 11 January 1917 and on 30 January *Derfflinger* ran out to the west with *Seydlitz* to meet returning Torpedoboote Flottilles. Further exercises in the German Bight followed on 3 March 1917. On 27 March *Derfflinger* began the trip to Kiel with the *Panzerkreuzers Von der Tann* and *Moltke*, arriving there that afternoon. Training including artillery shooting, night fighting training and war games in the so-called "Battle Picture". The return canal trip was made on 6 April. More picket duty, coaling and dockyard periods followed after the return to the North Sea.

On 16 May 1917 there were Fleet manoeuvres and on 13 June manoeuvres with *Seydlitz* in the Helgoland Bight, which were repeated on 29 June. Evolutions in the Helgoland Bight followed on 4 July and then that same day *von der Tann, Derfflinger* and *Moltke* made another trip through the Kaiser Wilhelm Canal to Kiel. Training in the Baltic continued until 23 July when the Unit made its way back to the North Sea. Picket duty was resumed.

On 18 August *Derfflinger* weighed anchor and escorted SMS *Baden* with His Majesty the Kaiser onboard on a trip into the German Bight to Helgoland before returning to Schillig Roads at

An aerial view of *Derfflinger* en-route from Wilhelmshaven to Kiel for repairs in June 1916, after the Skagerrak Battle

1920 hrs. The following day Fleet evolutions were carried. The general North Sea routine followed until 7 October when *Derfflinger* commenced the canal trip to Kiel as part of the I AG. Training in Kiel Bay and Mecklenburg Bay continued until 25 October when the return trip to the North Sea was begun.

On 2 November 1917 *Derfflinger* weighed anchor and steered down the Jade River with the battleships *Nassau* and *Rheinland* on a clear, bright moonlit night (*König Albert* and *Kaiserin* also took part). Their mission was to support minesweepers in the outer German Bight and act as security for a U-Boat convoy. For this operation *Derfflinger* had embarked a seaplane and at 1000 hrs aircraft 1532 was lowered to the water for reconnaissance, and then at 1300 hrs this Friedrichshafen FF49C aircraft was detached to List. Later Derfflinger returned to Schillig Roads. On 4 November the ship went into Wilhelmshaven Dockyard, for coaling among other things, before resuming picket duty on 9 November.

Derfflinger on Schillig Roads

On 12 November *Derfflinger* and *Moltke* gave further support to minesweepers, returning on the next day. On 18 November *Derfflinger* took part in a counter sweep by the I AG as Tactical Number 2 in the aftermath of the Battle in the Helgoland Bight on 17 November 1917.

On Friday 30 November *Derfflinger* undertook the canal trip to the Imperial Dockyard Kiel for the commencement of overhaul work. From 1 December until 26 December *Derfflinger* was out of service.

The final year of the war, 1918, began with evolutions in the German Bight on 8 January. Early on 23 January *Derfflinger* ran out for minesweeper security. Further support operations followed.

In March the work of supporting minesweepers continued. On 5 March *Derfflinger* and *Tann* ran out to cover minesweeper units, and evolutions followed on 14 March. A further canal trip to the east was begun on March 16 and *Derfflinger* arrived in Kiel the following day. On 18 March there was a slight collision with *Prinzregent Luitpold* in fog. From 19 March until 14 April *Derfflinger* lay in Floating Dock 7 for bow repairs. After completion of repair work the guns were adjusted on 15 April and the following day the trip back to the west was begun, arriving on Schillig Roads on 17 April. Further minesweeping support operations followed.

On 23 April *Derfflinger* ran out in the Unit of the I AG and in company with the entire High Sea Fleet for an operation to the coast of Norway, to intercept enemy forces covering convoy traffic between Norway and Scotland. There were no special events for *Derfflinger* and on 25 April the

Damage to *Derfflinger* during the Skagerrak Battle. Two bow armoured plates have been blown off

cruiser ran in on Route Blue and anchored on Wilhelmshaven Roads. Picket duty was resumed.

The next operation followed on 10 May when *Derfflinger* ran out with the I AG to the north. The Unit supported close behind the minesweepers until that evening they were replaced by the III Squadron. On 11 May *Derfflinger* returned to picket duty.

At 0230 hrs on 16 May *Derfflinger* ran out with *von der Tann* for the security of minesweepers. Nevertheless at 0345 hrs the Panzerkreuzer was rammed to starboard by the Sperrbrecher *Schwaben*. Four wing passage cells leaked and *Derfflinger* was detached back to the Jade River. At 1745hrs she passed through the lock of the III Entrance and at 1915hrs entered the floating dock. From 17 May until 29 May *Derfflinger* was under repair in the floating dock.

On 30 May *Derfflinger* ran out of dock and then departed for Brunsbüttel and the Baltic.

Training followed including a trip to the Kleinen Belt to familiarize commanders and Navigation Offizieres with this route. A period of training in Mecklenburg Bight followed, including battle training and shooting practice. On 17 June returned to the Jade. Picket duty was resumed.

On 22 June 1918 *Derfflinger* ran out in company with *Bayern* for minesweeper security, however, with a NW gale of force 6–8 minesweeping was impossible and a turn for home was made. The same occurred on 28 June, but this time there was a heavy swell. A short period in Wilhelmshaven harbour followed. On 7 July a further advance was made for the security of minesweepers, and was repeated the following day.

On 30 July 1918 the I AG put to sea under the leadership of Vizeadmiral Hipper. The object of the operation was to trial a new method of escorting U-Bootes out to sea through the mine belt by punching a hole through the minefields and allowing the U-Bootes to pass concurrently. The operation was a success and *Derfflinger* returned to Wilhelmshaven Roads only on 1 August.

On 11 August *Derfflinger* went to sea as security for minesweepers, however, when enemy forces were reported near Terschelling the minesweeping was broken off and *Derfflinger* returned to the Jade. Evolutions followed in the Helgoland Bight on 19 August. Once again *Derfflinger* ran out for minesweeper security on 29 August but the operation was called off when the poor weather precluded mine sweeping.

Evolutions in the Unit were conducted in the Helgoland Bight on 6 September and then the ships anchored at the Amrum anchorage. On 11 September *Derfflinger* went into the dockyard for boiler repairs, which continued until 15 September. More training for a Fleet operation followed. A further period of boiler repairs followed from 25 September until 1 October.

On 3 October 1918 *Derfflinger* ran out to sea in the Unit of the I AG as security for minesweepers before returning to Schillig Roads. More picket duty followed until 9 October when another minesweeper security operation took place. A further support operation on 24 October was called off because the minesweepers reported rough weather and therefore rangefinder training was carried out instead. On 26 October *Derfflinger* ran into Wilhelmshaven harbour for more work on the boilers and returned to Wilhelmshaven Roads on 29 October, ready for the planned operation against the Thames and Flanders coast. However, the operation was cancelled. On 30 October *Derfflinger* moved to Schillig Roads, before running into Wilhelmshaven on 31 October.

Derfflinger belonged to unit of ships which were interned at Scapa Flow and departed Wilhelmshaven on 19 November 1918. On 21 June 1919 the Panzerkreuzer was scuttled by her own crew and sank at 1445hrs. The cruiser lay in a depth of 27–30 metres keel up, with a list of 20°. Work to raise the wreck began in July 1938 but it was only a year later that *Derfflinger* was finally raised as the last German capital ship. She was towed behind Risa Island and remained there for seven years, floating bottom up, and no other ship has ever remained afloat upside down for so long. In 1946 *Derfflinger* was transferred to an ex-German floating dock and was towed to Faslane on the Clyde River. In just over 15 months *Derfflinger* was finally scrapped. On 30 August 1965 *Derfflinger's* ships bell was returned into German hands.

Images source: Gary Staff, German Battlecruisers of World War One, Seaforth Publishing 2014

Endnotes

1 These speeds were run in shallow water because of the war, and in deeper water speeds 2 knots higher could have been expected.

Derfflinger **in harbour after installation of a tripod mast**

SMS Derfflinger

Drawings: **Marsden Samuel**

HMS Furious
– the last of the large light cruisers

Jan Radziemski

Furious just after construction

Admiral Fisher had plans to build at least four Courageous-class *large light cruisers*. After he ordered the first two in the spring of 1915, he managed to get work started on the third unit as well. Unlike the other ships, this vessel would be armed with special calibre 457 mm (18 inches) cannons. Fisher chose them personally, without consulting the Bureau of Artillery first. *Furious*, like its two semi-sister units, was constructed specifically for the Baltic Project. The final version of the vessel was approved on May 23rd 1915.

Experts were even more sceptic about *Furious*'s armament than in the case of the two preceding units. Its main ordnance would be comprised of two calibre 457 mm BL18 cannons, built by Armstrong. Such heavy weapons were unprecedented at the time; the two guns represented the apex of the constant increase in British vessel guns calibres. Although cannons of such calibres had occasionally been installed in the previous century on battleships, they were obsolete, muzzle-loading designs. The new cannon's design was based on the BL15 Mk I, calibre 381 mm. Only three units have been produced (two for the vessel and one backup). The barrel was 40 calibres (or 35 according to other sources), and could be raised to an elevation of 30 degrees. The weight of each projectile was 1506 kg (3320 pounds). Muzzle velocity was 683 m/s when using normal propellants (286 kg / 631 pounds of Cordite MD) or 783 m/s if the more powerful variant of the propellant was used. In that case, and with maximum barrel elevation, the range of the gun was 32000 meters. The rate of fire was one round per minute. The guns were placed on two single-cannon Mk I turrets on the bow (position A) and on the stern (position Y). The enormous cannon weighed 148 tonnes (145.7 long tons), and the turret weighed 840 tonnes (826.7 long tons). Certain other sources give the weight of the turret at 1117 tonnes, or 1099.4 long tons. The turret alone had a crew of 67. The barbettes could also support two 15-inch cannon turrets, as on the two other vessels. To keep all this secret, in the official technical documentation, the cruiser's armament was listed as 15-inch cannons. Fire tests, performed in 1916, showed that the 18-inch cannon was essentially useless against sea targets, but the Admiralty maintained its decision about installing the ordnance on the new vessel. Naturally, Lord Fisher had intervened before this choice was made.

The stern turret (position Y) installed on the upper deck had a high barbette, which meant the barrel was located 8.53 meters above the normal water line. This was much higher than on *Courageous* and *Glorious*. During testing the cannon caused enormous vibrations, but the hull was not

Furious after entering service in 1917

damaged. However, *Furious* never got the chance to test its main gun in combat.

Furious was also fitted with new mid-range calibre artillery. Initially, eight 140 mm (5.5 inch) rapid-fire BL Mk I cannons with separate shells and propellant charges were planned; this number later increased to eleven. The calibre, rarely used by the Royal Navy, was first deployed on two cruisers built for Greece and later commandeered by the British (*Chester* and *Birkenhead*). The guns, designed in 1916 in Coventry, had a barrel length of 50 calibres and were installed on single Mk PI turrets. They had many advantages, including lighter projectiles, which made manual operation easier. Either armour-piercing or explosive rounds were used, with a weight of 37.19 kg (81.99 pounds) and a muzzle velocity 831 m/s. 11 kg (24.25 pounds) of Cordite MD were used as the charge. With the barrel raised to thirty degrees, the guns were able to attain a range of 16250 meters. The rate of fire was 12 rounds per minute. Each cannon had two hundred rounds assigned: 120 armour-piercing rounds, 64 explosive rounds and 16 armour-piercing tracer rounds. The firing position with the protective cover weighed 18878 kg (41618.9 pounds). Initially, the ship's anti-aircraft armament were two calibre 76mm QF 3 guns, installed forward of the funnel. When the unit entered service, it had four such guns installed. Like her sister ships, *Furious* was also fitted with two underwater 533 mm torpedo tubes in front of the bow turret barbette, with ten torpedoes each. The ship also had mine-laying devices installed on the stern, but no sea mines were ever loaded onto the vessel.

To direct artillery fire, two rangefinders with a base of 4.57 meters installed on the stern artillery turret "Y" and on the roof of the command post were used. A further two rangefinders with a base of 2.74 meters were installed on the stern torpedo command post and the bow fire command post. On the bow quarterdeck, a 2 meter rangefinder for directing anti-aircraft fire was fitted.

Armour

Furious had similar armour as her sister ships. The only difference was in the main artillery turret armour thickness: the front and side plates were 229 mm thick, the rear one 208 mm, and the roof 127 mm. All plates were made of reinforced Krupp armoured steel. The extra hull width was used for anti-torpedo bulges, which were integrated into the hull. Adjacent to them were anti-torpedo watertight doors, which ran along the entire length of the hull.

Power

The ship was powered by four Brown-Curtis steam turbine units, manufactured by Wallsend Slipway & Engineering. Each unit had a low and high pressure turbine, as well as a reverse turbine. Power was transmitted from the turbines by single stage gearboxes to four shafts, each ending with screw with a diameter of 3.5 meters. Steam was generated in 18 Yarrow water-tube boilers. Theoretically, the engines were capable of producing 90000 HP. The Admiralty decided a speed of 31.5 knots would be satisfactory. The vessel

Tab. 1. Dates of construction

The name of the ship	Shipyard	Keel laid on	Launched on	Commissioned to the fleet on
„Furious"	Armstrong Whitworth in Newcastle upon Tyne	08.06.1915	18.08.1916	04.07.1917

carried 762 tonnes of fuel, though its total tank capacity was 3211 tonnes. Fully loaded, the ship had a range of 6900 sea miles at a speed of 20 knots.

Other equipment

The vessel was fitted with 9 headlights with a diameter of 91.4 cm. One was installed under the bow foremast, two on the bridge behind the command post, two on the platform on the frontal section of the funnel and four on the main mast platform. *Furious*'s emergency equipment was as follows: two motor boats, 11 meters long, cutters, two rescue boats having 9.8 meters in length each, two boats having 9.15 meters in length, two whaleboats having 8.24 meters in length, two gigs having 9.15 meters in length, two yawls having 4.9 meters in length and two wooden balsa rafts, 4.1 meters long each.

Crew

The ship's designed initially assumed a crew of 726. After completion, it was determined that a crew of 737 would be required. Other sources claim that the vessel entered service with a crew of 880, including 84 airmen.

Construction and trials

Furious was laid down on June 8th 1915 in the Armstrong Whitworth shipyard in Wallsend. The ship was launched on August 15th (according to other sources: August 18th) 1916. At launch, the cruiser weighed 12680 tonnes, with a hull weight of 9892 tonnes. At the time the war was entering a decisive stage, and the Admiralty's priorities began to change. The role of the air force was slowly beginning to be appreciated. Most likely, this is why on March 19th 1917 the Admiralty decided to alter the project and transform *Furious* into an aircraft carrier. Three designs had been prepared. Ultimately, it was decided that the bow section of the hull would house the flight deck and that a hangar for 8-10 reconnaissance and fighter aircraft would be built. Naturally, this meant that there was no room left for the bow artillery turret. The changes took 11 months to complete and after 2 years since the beginning of construction, on June 26th 1917, the ship was ready for its trials. Because of the war situation no official trials were held, but at the suggestion of the shipyard, the vessel made a few trial runs, attaining a speed of 30 knots and developing 90820 HP. On July 4th 1917 the vessel was incorporated into the fleet. The exact construction cost isn't known, as only the cost of the hull was given (1050000 pounds sterling). The first commander of *Furious* was Wilmot S. Nicholson. In the Royal Navy's long-running history, this was the fifth vessel with that name. Her Latin motto, borrowed from Virgil, was *furor arma ministrat – rage supplies arms.*

Conversion

Furious entered service as a hybrid vessel, with a different silhouette than her semi-sister units. Her bow flight deck became her most distinctive feature. The 69.5 by 15.2 meters flight deck, tilted

Tower 'Y,' calibre 457 mm at the stern

Large light cruiser *Furious* in its full glory

towards the bow, was used by aircraft and seaplanes only for take-offs. Landing on such a short runway required a lot of expertise. In order to secure aircraft parked on the flight deck during bad weather, a special fence was constructed across and in the bow section of the flight deck. The barrier could be stowed if necessary. Below the flight deck, a hangar was constructed; its dimensions were 36.6 by 18.3 by 4.7 meters, and it could house 10 aircraft, although initially only 8 were stationed on the ship: 3 Short 184 reconnaissance units and 5 Sopwith Pup fighters with wheeled undercarriage. In the back of the hangar two electric lifts were installed for transporting aircraft up to 9 by 5 meters. The ship was also fitted with a repair garage and 600 two-gallon barrels of fuel. The ammunition hold was used to store bombs.

The only change in ordnance was the removal of the bow 457 mm cannon. The ship was still fitted with eleven 140 mm guns and two anti-aircraft 76 mm cannons.

Seaplanes took off using special four-wheeled carts, moving along a special guide bar installed along the deck. Landing was done on water; aircraft were then lifted onto the deck using two booms. Naturally, bad weather conditions or enemy presence posed major problems with this system. In such cases, seaplanes were picked up by smaller units, *Nairana* or *Pegasus*. Regular aircraft normally headed to land-based airstrips after completing their mission. This significantly reduced the operational range of the vessel. After *Furious* entered service, a large number of experiments on take-off and landing was conducted. A new strategy for landing on the flight deck, developed by Squadron Commander Dunning, was tested. The plane would circle the vessel before attempting to land, waiting for it to attain the needed speed. When the ship's speed matched that of the aircraft, it would suspend itself above the flight deck, while the crew would pull it down onto the deck using wires attached to it. On August 2nd 1917 Dunning was able to successfully land his plane twice using this technique. However, on August 7th the landing went wrong: the engine stalled and the airplane was blown overboard, killing the pilot. Because of this further experiments were cancelled, and on October 17th it was decided that the ship would undergo further changes: the flight deck would be expanded and an additional stern hangar would be built. The renovation works were performed between December 1917 and March 1918.

In December, the ship arrived at the shipyard. The first step was to remove the main mast and the stern artillery turret. These changes were strongly opposed by some of the more conservative admirals. The structures were replaced with a 91.4 by 21.3 m flight deck. Under the deck a hangar (35.4 by 10.1 by 4.6 m) was built. Between the hangar and the flight deck ran a lift with a maximum load of 3 tonnes. The hangar was also fitted with a repair garage. In this configuration, the vessel was capable of carrying 16 aircraft, although from time to time as many as 26 units were on board. The two flight decks were connected by narrow ramps (3.35 meters), built along the sides, next to the quarterdeck and the funnel. This enabled the crew to move planes between the flight decks with the help of special carts, which used tracks built into the ramps. The stern flight deck was fit-

Tab. 2 . Basic characteristics of HMS *Furious*	
Displacement (t)	
- light (empty)	18480
- normal	19513
- full	22890
Dimensions (m)	
- overall length	239,8
- length between perpendiculars	224,09
- Maximum beam	26,84
- draught (at full displacement)	7,49
Metacentric height at full/deep displacement (m)	1,14/1,62
Hull height from keel to upper deck (m)	
- at bow part	9,14
- amidships	4,88
- at stern part	4,27

Note: according to R.A. Burt the initial project stated that at normal displacement 19100 tonnes HMS *Furious* was to be 224 m long (length between perpendiculars) (according to S. Breyer -228,6 m), the overall length was to be 240,0 m (according to Conway 239,7 m, S. Breyer – 239,8 m); the beam - 26,82 m, draught at bow 6,24 m, at stern 6,86 m.

Furious view from the stern quarter

ted with ropes, which were then hooked by a landing aircraft and allowed it to slow down. The idea was rather simple: each rope had bags of sand attached at the other and. As this system wasn't particularly reliable, at the end of the runway a special elastic barrier built out of Manila ropes was constructed, capable of stopping a plane before it crashed into the funnel.

Despite these changes the vessel still retained its anti-aircraft guns and 10 calibre 140 mm cannons. As with her sister ships, torpedo ordnance was improved: four triple 533 mm torpedo tubes were installed above water line. According to certain sources, this number was even greater: six or as many as eight triple tubes.

Another upgrade did not solve all the problems pertaining to the aerial operations on board the vessel. Air turbulences caused by hot fumes coming out of the funnel and the superstructure made it difficult for the light air planes to land on the deck, which often resulted in failures and crashes. The number of landings on the aft deck had to be reduced until the next rebuilding of the ship. HMS *Furious* was at the moment used in reconnaissance missions utilising small observation balloons. After the end of the war, at the early twenties of the twentieth century, a decision was made to modernise the ship once again. It took place in the years 1922-1925.

Here follows a little information about the fate of the guns removed from HMS *Furious* after her modernisations. Two of them (the bow gun and the stern gun) were installed in 1918 on board the Lord Clive-class monitors: HMS General Wolfe and HMS Lord Clive. The guns were placed on the aft deck with their barrels fixed to face the starboard side. The monitors were used to provide shelling of the coast and they carried out the duty very well. After both monitors were scrapped, their cannons were preserved in Royal Navy armouries until 1933, when they were scrapped as well. Some sources mention that they were transferred to the Singapore base to strengthen its coastal defences. In 1942, after the surrender of the base, they allegedly fell into Japanese hands. The third cannon was to be installed on board the monitor HMS Prince Eugene, but after the end of the war it was taken to the artillery range in Siloth, where, after being fitted with a new reduction tube (downsizing the calibre to 406 mm), it was used for testing new heavy naval cannons.

Tab. 3. Basic artillery characteristics

Details for	BL 18 in Mk I	BL 5,5 in Mk I
Calibre (mm)	457	139,7
Turret/mount mass (t)	840*	18,87
Gun mass (t)	148	6,3
Barrel length (mm)	18293	6985
Barrel length (in calibres)	40**	50
Charge type	MD 45	MD 19
Charge mass (kg)	286	11,0/10,2
Cartridge mass (kg)	1506	37,19
Initial speed of a projectile (m/s)	683/783	831/850
Range (m/gun elevation, degrees)	32000/30°	16250/30°

* according other data 1117 tonnes
** according other data 35 calibres

Battlecruiser HMS *Incomparable*

The progress achieved in Lord Fisher's era resulted in the increase of the main artillery calibre from 307 mm to 457 mm. Nevertheless even that was not enough for the admiral. During roughly the same time when our three cruisers were being built, Fisher was working on a new project. Its cul-

Furious after second update with two aircraft decks

mination point were the concept of HMS Incomparable presented in the spring of 1915, which was finally rejected by the Admiralty Council. The battlecruiser was to be armed with 6 guns of an uncommon calibre 508 mm and she was to achieve absolute superiority over any other known ships of the line. The middle artillery, already being used on board HMS Renown and HMS Courageous was supplemented with anti-aircraft guns and torpedo tubes. The hefty power plant with installed power of 180000 shp was to give the colossus the speed of 35 knots. Not much more is known about this kind of vessels aside the fact that they were to be the continuation of the Renown-class battlecruisers and Courageous-class large light cruisers.

In service

Entering the service by HMS Courageous and HMS Glorious was a headache for the Admiralty. After the fiasco of the Baltic Project, after Fisher had left the post of the First Lord of Admiralty, nobody had any idea how to use his ships in action. As for HMS *Furious*, with her hybrid version, the situation was quite different. Despite all the critical remarks coming from specialists, seamen and pilots, the ship had very precise tasks to perform and proved to be more useful than other seaplane carriers HMS Campania, Engadine and Riviera. Those ships and the likes had hangars for a few seaplanes but were not fitted with a landing deck which greatly deteriorated their operational potential – their seaplanes could take off and land on the sea surface only during periods of good weather conditions.

Soon after being commissioned into the Grand Fleet HMS *Furious* raised the flag of the Sea Air Force Commander. Performing different kinds of tests and fixing minor malfunctions occurred until November 1917. The ship took part in a handful of sea patrols in the North Sea region in August and September of 1917. On October 16th, she went to sea in search of two German light cruisers Brummer and Bremse, which planned to attack a British convoy carrying iron ore from Bergen to Lerwick. HMS *Furious* was soon joined by HMS Courageous and HMS Glorious. Admiral David Beatty – Commander of the Grand Fleet – sent almost all the light vessels in his disposal to join the cruisers. Despite such a full-scale search the Germans were capable to slip past the British task forces and attack the convoy, sinking 9 of 12 of its ships and 2 escorting destroyers. After completing their mission, the German cruisers reached safely their home base.

In March 1918 HMS *Furious* went to sea trials after her second modernisation. The ship was commissioned as an aircraft carrier and managed to take part in the war before it ended. On June 17th 1918, HMS *Furious* was attacked by two German seaplanes which managed to drop their bombs, luckily without hitting their target. Two Sopwith Camel fighter planes took off the deck but they were unable to intercept the attackers. As the result the fighters were forced to land on the sea surface and were irretrievably lost. On the very same day another German seaplanes attacked the ship. This time the Camels proved to be more effective and downed one enemy aircraft, again losing two machines, which were forced to ditch in the sea. The balance was therefore unfavourable for the British: they lost four planes to down only one German machine. After that event the ship's anti-aircraft defence was strengthened by installing 2 (3?) 76 mm flak guns.

On June 19th 1918, seven of the ship's planes attacked the German airship base located on Jutland Peninsula. As the result of the air raid two German airships L-54 and L-60 were destroyed. Problems started when the planes attempted to land on the deck of their ship. Three machines were destroyed while landing on the sea surface near the ship. Three others went to the neutral Danish airfields where their pilots were interned. One plane was missing. It must be added, though, that until the end of the war not a single plane managed to land on the deck of HMS *Furious*.

Epilogue

Thanks to his energy, tenacity and persuasive skills, Lord Fisher managed to implement his plan – while straining the public finances — of building a series of big and strange ships which nobody knew how to use. The admiral himself once again retired, leaving the problem for his friends in Admiralty to solve. Luckily, an era of aircraft carriers was slowly dawning. Thanks to that „the old man's children" – as Winston Churchill used to name the ships – became something no reasonable person dare to question any more. The first one to undergo such a metamorphosis was HMS *Furious*.

But this is, as they say, another story.

Source of pictures: Royal Navy, Imperial War Museum, National Maritime Museum.

Endnotes

1. With this end in view Fisher ordered two pairs of 381 mm guns, but they were not yet ready in the spring of 1915.
2. Some sources claim that in November 1917 they were replaced for 102 mm guns.
3. According to other data 27 for 15,5 m and height – 4,3 m.
4. According to T. Klimczyk the ship had no equipment to raise the seaplanes on board.
5. According to other data the length of the board was 86,4 m.
6. Armstrong Shipyard presented to the Admiralty the plans of complete modernisation of HMS Furious with a full-length board for planes. The same project included telescopic funnel and navigation cabin that could be hidden inside the hull.

Bibliography

S. Breyer, *Schlachtschiffe Und Schlachtkreuzer 1905-1970*, Karl Müller Verlag, München 1996.

R. A. Burt, *British Battleships of World War One*, Annapolis, Naval Institute Press, 1986.

Coway's All the world's fighting ships 1906-1921, Conway Maritime Press Ltd. London 1992.

T. Klimczyk, *HMS Furious (I)*, „Morza, Statki i Okręty" nr 3/1996

T. Klimczyk, *Białe sonie. Courageous, Glorious, Furious*, Warszawa 1999.

W. B. Mużenikow, *Liniejnyje kriejsiera Anglii: Czast IV*. Istfłot. Samara 2006.

O. Parkes, *British Battleships, „Warrior" 1860 to „Vanguard" 1950: a History of Design, Construction and Armament*, Leo Cooper. London 1990.

J. Roberts, *Battlecruisers*, Naval Institute Press. Annapolis 1997.

T. Wywerka Prekurat, *Białe słonie*, „Morze" nr 11/1972.

Monitor *Lord Clive* with the powerful cannon 457 mm at the stern

HMS Furious

Furious's appearance according to original design

Drawings: **Dmitriy Solomatin**

Furious's appearance after entering service

The battles of the Italian submarine fleet in the Mediterranean Sea in 1942

Marek Sobski

Submarine minelayer *Pietro Micca* anchored in Taranto, 1942 [Photo *Storia Militare Dossier No. 11*]

In January 1942, the Axis armed forces in Africa took the offensive. Fuel was transported to Africa among others by Italian submarines. The downside of this solution was that it only added its share to toxic and dangerous fumes omnipresent on-board those ships. To reduce this threat, the submarines often had to remain emerged while travelling, thus allowing the crews to properly ventilate the ships.

Fuel for Rommel

On January 4th, the *sommergibile* (submarine) 'Saint Bon' under captain Gustavo Miniero set off from Taranto to Tripoli. Its cargo was almost 155 tons of fuel and ammunition. On her way, the ship was to refuel in Palermo. During the night 'Saint Bon' crossed the Strait of Messina and at dawn on January 5th, she reached the longitude of the Cape of Milazzo. There she was spotted by the British submarine HMS Upholder. The captain of the British vessel, Commander Lieutenant M. D. Wanklyn ordered an emergency dive and through the periscope determined the origin of the spotted vessel. Miniero also managed to spot the British submarine but for unknown reasons he did not give any order to dive. Instead he took a turn while in full speed. The British did not intend to miss such an opportunity. They launched two torpedoes: the first one, launched at 05.39 from a distance of 800 metres, missed its target; the second, launched at 5.42, covered the distance in 35 seconds and exploded at the portside of the Italian ship, close to her bow cannon[1]. 'Saint Bon' sank immediately, 8nm from the aforementioned cape. Only a few members of her crew, who were standing in the conning tower during the attack, survived. After 10 minutes HMS Upholder resurfaced and took three castaways, one of which happened to be an officer on watch. These lucky people were *sottotenente di vascello* Luigi Como, *sergente silurista* Valentino Ceccon and *capo silurista* Ernesto Fiore. Along with the ship died her captain, seven other officers and 49 petty officers and seamen.

On January 30th, 1942 another Italian submarine *Medusa* was lost (commanded by *capitano di corvetta* Enrico Bertarelli). The ship had been assigned to *Scuola Sommergibili* in Pula, and was

returning from her training voyage to the Bay of Kotor (between the Isle of Cres and the Istra coast). There were 60 people on-board the ship during the attack; among them 6 officers and 21 petty officers and seamen who took part in the training. *Medusa* was accompanied by a steamer *Grado*, another submarine *Mameli* and an old torpedo boat *Insidioso*. At 14.10, at the longitude of the Cape of Promontore, she was hit by one of the four torpedoes launched from a distance of one kilometre by the British submarine *HMS Thorn*. The Italian vessels managed to outmanoeuvre the other three. *Medusa* went down merely in 10 seconds, at 44°45' N and 13°36' E (about a kilometre away from the Isle of Fenera). Seven members of her crew, officers only (together with the captain of the vessel), managed to stay afloat. The steamer *Carlo Zeno* took up three wounded men, one of whom, *guardiamarina* Arturo Fei, died in hospital in Pula. The remaining 53 members of the crew went to the bottom with their ship. Some of them (14 people) still remained alive, trapped inside the aft part of the hull. They managed to contact the rescue party with the help of a telephone buoy. The rescue operation that followed was unsuccessful due to bad weather conditions.

In January 1942, in the event of the Axis offensive in Africa, Regia Marina carried out two major supply operations –'M 43' and 'T18'. The British also sent two convoys from Alexandria to Malta. Italian submarines operated off the coast of Malta and along the line between the island of Gavdos and the Benghazi coast, other regions were not being patrolled. In the first days of January, during the 'M 43' operation, Italian submarines *Axum, Turchese, Aradam, Platino, Onice, Delfino* and *Alagi* took positions near Malta, while *Galatea, Beilul* and *Dessiè* operated a little further to the east. Between 22nd and 25th January, during the 'T 18' operation, the submarines *Squalo, Narvalo, Santarosa, Topazio, Platino* and *Corallo* took their positions in the vicinity of the Maltan archipelago and in the Sicilian Canal, while *Galatea, Ametista* and *Turchese* were waiting in the region between Ras Aamer and Tobruk. Six cargo missions were also undertaken.

In February 1942, 24 Italian submarines completed merely 31 missions. They operated mainly in the central and eastern part of the Mediterranean. Their actions were the result of the Italian 'K 7' operation, that is a convoy to Libya, and the British 'MF 5' supply operation for Malta. Between 15th and 24th February submarines *Alagi, Brin, Axum, Aradam* and *Turchese* were operating on Tunisian and Algerian waters. *Santarosa, Narvalo* and *Mocenigo* were patrolling the region close to Malta. Between 10th and 13th February, *Menotti, Ondina, Tricheco, Topazio, Sirena, Dandolo, Malachite, Platino* and *Perla*, took positions at the Cyrenaica coast, sweeping the area of 800 square miles. Their task was to act counter to the 'MF 5,' already under way. In addition, two submarines *Beilul* and *Dagabur* were operating along the Syrian-Palestinian coast between the 13th and 19th February. In February 1942, *Topasio* (commanded by *capitano di corvetta* Bruno Zelik) attacked an enemy destroyer with no effect.

Two photos of the vessel *Bandiera* as it appeared while part of the *Scuola Sommergibili* in Pola, 1942 [Photo *Storia Militare Dossier No. 11*]

Triumphs of the British submariners

In the first half of March 1942, the Italians carried out a convoy operation 'V 5.' Two cargo vessels were escorted by a large group of floating vessels and five submarines, placed in positions east of Malta, whose task was to engage the ships trying to attack the convoy. One of the submarines was *Ammiraglio Millo* (under *capitano di corvetta* Vincenzo Amato), which since the 6th of March operated south of Malta[2]. The ship did not spot any

Delfino in 1942, with its sail newly renovated [Photo *Storia Militare Dossier No. 11*]

enemies, so according to the plan *Millo* she headed home on the 12th of March.

Millo was on her way to Taranto, and had just reached Cape Stilo when at 13.23 on March 14th, she was attacked by the British submarine *HMS Ultimatum* commanded by Lieutenant Peter R.H. Harrison. The Italian vessel remained surfaced, zigzagging. The British launched a full salvo of torpedoes from the bow launchers, and two of them hit the Italian vessel in the stern and midship sections. *Millo* sank immediately at 38°27' N and 16°37' E. The Italians noticed the torpedo trails and therefore many of them managed to jump into the water. Among the rescued members of the crew were the first officer *tenente di vascello* Marcello Bertini, three other officers and ten petty officers and seamen. Luckily, all of them were taken captive by the British. In addition, *sergente elettricista* Lingua was rescued at 14.08 by a boat, whose crew had seen the whole event from the shore and came to rescue. 57 people died, including the ship's captain.[3]

At about 6.00 on March 17th. *Guglielmotti*, previously operating on the Red Sea and the Atlantic, was sunk by HMS *Unbeaten*, 15 Mm south from Cape Spartivento (at 37°42' N and 15°38' E). The Italian vessel had left Taranto for Cagliari two days earlier. All her crew - the captain *tenente di vascello* Federico Tamburini, 6 other officers, 54 petty officers and seamen — sank with the ship.

At 17.30 on March 18th the submarine *Tricheco*" (under *capitano di corvetta* Giovanni Cunsolo) was sunk by another British vessel - *HMS Upholder*. The Italians were going on the surface from Augusta to Brindisi, they were just about 4 nm from their destination, where their ship was to undergo a technical check. *Tricheco* was hit in the bow section by a single torpedo, which cut her in two parts and quickly sent to the bottom. Among the dead were first officer *tenente di vascello* Ermanno Tonti and 37 petty officers and seamen. The ship's captain and ten of his subordinates managed to save their lives.

In the very same month, the Italian fleet also noted some small successes. Around March 15th, *Mocenigo* and *Dandolo* operated off the coast of North Africa. The first vessel sank on March 14th — a tanker (5000 BRT) near Cape Carbon. On March 16th, 35 nm from Beirut, *Galatea* (under *tenente di vascello* Mario Baroglio) sank a Greek barge *Zoodochos Pighi* (170 BRT) transporting fuel. The ship was fired upon with a cannon, her crew was allowed to lower the rescue boats, then the Italians came closer and sank the barge with planted explosives. In the meantime they spotted an escort ship, searching for enemy submarines. *Galatea* approached her and attacked with a single torpedo, without any effects.

Between the 7th and 11th of March 1942, the Italians carried out a supply operation 'V 5' for the troops in Africa. Three supply missions for Malta were also carried out by the British. In March, Italian *sommergibili* carried out merely 20 missions, which was the lowest number of missions from the beginning of the war. During the period of March 27th–29th, *Aradam*, *Turchese*, *Santarosa* and *Narvalo* were patrolling the Sicilian Canal, intending to engage the ships from the British Force 'H' from Gibraltar, which were delivering planes to Malta. *Corallo*, *Millo* and '*Veniero* were positioned south of Malta. On March 18th, *Onice* and *Platino* took positions south-west of Gavdos Island and

Ruggiero Settimo leaving Pola in 1942 (Photo *Storia Militare Dossier No. 11*)

Jalea in the sea in 1942 [Photo *Storia Militare Dossier No. 11*]

were attacked by enemy planes and a submarine. The two vessels reported sighting a convoy, which had been moving towards Malta since March 20th. The Supermarina command decided to take actions which led to the Second Battle of Syrta. At that time *Ametista* and *Galatea* were patrolling the area south of Cyprus.

On April 5th 1942, *HMS Havock* left Malta to single-handedly reach Gibraltar. On April 6th, east of Cap Bon (Tunisia) an Italian submarine *Aradam* (under *tenente di vascello* Oscar Gran) spotted the British destroyer going west towards Cap Bon. At 03.17, remaining on the surface, the submarine managed to hit the enemy with a torpedo fired from a distance of 500 m. The destroyer, badly damaged and on fire, tried to run aground but when her ammunition exploded, she broke in half. The scene was being watched from *Aradam* remaining on the surface. The whole event seems to be a little enigmatic – according to another version, the British destroyer ran aground without being hit by the Italian submarine. They did not manage to set the ship free and that was why the crew abandoned their vessel and were interned by the French. The abandoned ship was hit by a torpedo from *Aradam*. The position was at 36°48' N and 11°08' E. In the third version, it is speculated that the destroyer could have run aground while trying to evade a torpedo. While stuck aground, the vessel was destroyed by her own crew.

In April 1942, first *Brin*, *Veniero* and *Argo*, and later in the month *Emo* and *Velella* operated in the western part of the Mediterranean Sea. *Turchese* and *Aradam* were sent in the Cap Bon region, and then replaced by *Onice* and *Corallo*. The latter, under the command of *tenente di vascello* Gino Andreani, on April 28th, sank two Tunisian barges remaining in the restricted area without permission required from Vichy vessels. The small barges, *Dar es Salaam* (138 BRT) and *Tunis* (41 BRT) ran into the patrolling submarine and were fired upon and sunk at 37°01' N and 11°09' E. In the third decade of the month, the coast of Cyrenaica was being patrolled by *Accaio* and *Perla*, later by *Malachite* and *Uarsciek* , and finally by *Ondina* and *Sirena*. *Nereide* patrolled the Aegean Sea north of the Cyclades between the 5th and the 15th of April. 'H2' and 'H8' went for a night mission on April 22nd, 23rd and 30th, searching for enemy submarines in the Taranto Bay. 21 vessels completed 22 missions.

The Tragedy of *Antoniotto Usodimare*

Between April 29th and May 25th 1942, during the 'G.A.4' operation, the submarine *Ambra* delivered three human torpedoes in the region of Alexandria. The whole operation was unsuccessful, the divers sank their 'maials' and were captured by the British. One of the Italians managed to stay in hiding in Alexandria for the whole month of May before he was captured.

Ondina in 1942. The renovated conning tower, much smaller than previously, can be seen in the second picture [Photo *Storia Militare Dossier No. 11*]

A *classe 600* vessel, probably *Aradam*, anchored in Cagliari, 1942 [Photo *Storia Militare Dossier No. 11*]

The constant and rising threat were allied planes – *Argo* was attacked three times from the air in the short period between 22nd and 29th of May 1942, and had to spend three months in a dock.

In the evening of May 17th, *Veniero* (under *tenente di vascello* Elio Zappetta) left Cagliari and set off for the designated region south of the Balearic Islands. The last communique from this vessel was received on May 29th, at 16.25. *Veniero* reported spotting an enemy vessel; the next message, sent at 23.30, was unable to decode. The ship was likely to have been lost due to enemy's actions between May 29th and the first days of June 1942. After the war, it was determined that a vessel identified as an Italian submarine had been attacked early in the morning of June 7th by a Catalin seaplane, somewhere between Majorca and Sardinia. The attack had been resumed around noon that day, and the vessel — not submerged and likely damaged – had been sunk. The ship in question was most probably *Veniero*. Her subjugator was R.M. Corrie from Australia, the pilot of the Catalin from the 202 Squadron.[4] *Veniero* was sunk with her captain, five other officers and 52 petty officers and seamen.

Another Italian submarine patrolling in the region was *Argo* – repeatedly attacked by British planes, she defended herself with AA guns, hitting some attackers. Despite some damages the ship managed to return to base.

In May 1942, 22 Italian submarines completed 24 missions. The region south of the Balearic Islands was patrolled by *Mocenigo*, *Otaria*, *Turchese* and *Dessiè*, which were replaced by *Brin*, *Veniero* and *Argo*. Only *Mocenigo*, on May 18th, managed to attack – without any effect — enemy ships which had left Gibraltar and were heading for Malta to supply the island with new planes. *Uarsciek* and *Perla* operated along the Tunisian coasts and in the Sicilian Canal, to be replaced first by *Corallo* and *Aradam*, and then by *Alagi*. The eastern part of the Mediterranean was patrolled first by *Galatea* and *Nereide*, and then by *Asteria*, *Platino* and *Beilul*.

In June, ancient *Enrico Totti* left *Scuola Sommergibili* in Pula (she had been assigned there on March 1st 1941) and completed three supply missions, carrying urgent supplies to Libya, taking around 65 tons at a time.

Early in the morning of June 7th, in the region of Bizerta, *Corallo* used her cannon to sink the

Topazio returning to base after training [Photo *Storia Militare Dossier No. 11*]

Bajamonti (previously *Smeli*, a Jugoslavian vessel) as it appeared in 1942. Renovation works had been completed shortly before, after its acquisition [Photo *Storia Militare Dossier No. 11*]

barge *Hady M'Hamed* (26 BRT), suspected of helping the enemy. Six crew members were taken on-board the submarine.

At around 21.20 on June 8th 1942, *Alagi* (under *tenente di vascello* Sergio Puccini) mistakenly launched three torpedoes towards a friendly destroyer *Antoniotto Usodimare* (under *capitano di fregata* Luigi Merini). When hit, the destroyer broke in half and went down in five minutes, 72 nm north from Cap Bon. Of 306 crew members 141 were killed and 165 rescued. The destroyer was part of the convoy *Alagi* had not been notified of due to various communication mistakes. The convoy consisted of a motor ship *Vettor Pisani* and a few escort ships from Regia Marina. *Usodimare* left Naples at around 02.00 on June 8th, and the convoy headed for Tripoli. It was the sole example of sinking an Italian destroyer by a friendly vessel. Puccini must be excused though, as he had received clear information that each and every ship in his region would be an enemy vessel.

Between 9th and 22nd of June *Zaffiro* (under *tenente di vascello* Carlo Mottura) was lost under unknown circumstances. A day before she had left the port in Cagliari and headed for the region 50 nm south from Cape Salinas on the Majorca. As a result of the *Harpoon* operation, the ship, along with *Bronzo*, *Emo* and *Velella*, was to take position between the capes of Falcon and Ferrat in the Oran region. The order probably never reached *Zeffiro*. No further communiques were received from the ship despite many attempts to re-establish communication, made until July 22nd. It was not until in the 80s when a missing ship was identified in the pictures taken by an allied plane. It is likely that the submarine was attacked as early as on June 9th by a *PBY Catalina* flying boat from RAF 240. Squadron (piloted by Flight Lieutenant D. E. Hawkins). The plane was flying from Great Britain to India, doing a patrolling duty on its way. Its crew spotted an emerged submarine, commenced the attack and met with intensive AA fire. The bombs might have fatally damaged the ship, her crew members manning the AA gun were also fired upon. In the meantime a second Catalin (piloted by Flight Officer Godber) came for help and dropped eight depth charges set for 15 metres. *Zaffiro* submerged for a moment, then resurfaced, clearly damaged and dead in the water. Her crew went on-board with the intention to surrender and then the ship sank (at 38°03' N and 04°00' E or 38°21' N and 03°21' E). Hawkins[5] tried to land in order to save the crew, but the rough sea damaged his floats and effectively made the attempt impossible. The ship sank about 35 nm south-west of Ibiza. The entire crew perished – the captain, four other officers and 42 petty officers and seamen[6]. Also, contemporary sources often cite incorrectly that on June 24th 1942, the British submarine *HMS Ultimatum* (under Commander Peter R. H. Harrison) sank *Zaffiro*.

During the *Harpoon* operation (June 11th-16th) *Uarsciek* commenced an unsuccessful attempt to attack the enemy. Five *Adua* type ships were positioned, among other vessels, along the presumed route of the convoy. In June, Italian submarines completed 53 missions. *Brin* and *Malachite* patrolled the coastal waters of Algeria, replaced by *Giada*, *Acciaio*, *Corallo* and *Aradam*, the latter operating also in the vicinity of the Balearic Islands. Since June 6th *Velella*, *Zaffiro* and *Alagi* appeared on the Tunisian waters. Since June 15th *Dessiè*, *Aradam*, *Bronzo*, *Otaria*, *Corallo*, *Ascianghi*, *Axum*, *Atropo*, *Micca*, *Zoea* and *Platino* took positions around Malta. Some of them was attacked by enemy planes and ships. *Giada* and *Uarsciek* attacked the ships from the *Harpoon* convoy, with no effect. *Ascianghi* and *Onice* were sent to counteract the enemy formation returning to the Gibraltar base. At the end of the month *Dessiè*, *Onice* and *Axum* operated between the Sicilian Canal and Malta. At the time the western part of the Mediterranean was being patrolled by *Emo*, *Malachite*,

Onice and *Bajamonti* anchored, 1942 [Photo *Storia Militare Dossier No. 11*]

Port of *Poli, Encrico Toti* is returning from a training cruise. In the background, the tender of the sommergibili *Quarnerolo* (previously the Jugoslavian *Hvar*) can be seen. Early January 1942 [Photo *Storia Militare Dossier No. 11*]

Giada, *Velella* and *Uarsciek*. *Beilul*, *Sirena*, *Ondina* and *Galatea* counteracted the *Vigorous* operation. The Italian submarines again undertook supply missions: *Micca* and *Zoea* delivered to Derna and Benghazi 240, 5 tons of supplies (mainly fuel and tiny amounts of food). In the first half of

The demise of legendary *Scire*

On June 6th, 1942, the *sommergibile Perla* (*tenente di vascello* Gioacchino Ventura) left for Cyprus, its patrol area. On July 9th, off the coast of Beirut, *Perla* was traveling on the surface when it encountered *HMS Hyacint*. The submersible opened fire, but the British were able to avoid the torpedo and counterattack. The Italian vessel sustained such damage that the crew was forced to resurface, commence an emergency self-destruction procedure, and abandon ship. However, *Perla* was sinking slowly, and an armed British boarding party from the *Hyacint* managed to board the ship and prevent it from sinking. The corvette towed the damage submersible to Beirut, where it joined the ranks of the Royal Navy as the *P 712*. After tests were conducted, *Perla* was sold to the Greek Navy, where it served until 1954 as *Matrozos*. Sergeant Antonio De Maria was the only one to die in that day's events; the rest were taken prisoners.

On July 9th 1942, around 8 p.m., *Alagi* (*tenente di vascello* Sergio Puccini) sank *Antares* (3723 BRT), a Turkish tanker chartered from the British, with two torpedoes. The attack happened near the port of Tripola, at 34°59' N 35°32' E.

On July 11th 1942, two South African trawlers, *Walrus* and *Southern Maid*, with the help of British aircraft, sank the Italian submarine *Ondina* (*tenente di vascello* Gabriele Andolfi) south of Cyprus. The submarine was heavily damaged by the attack, and forced to resurface. *Ondina* encountered the enemy around 2 p.m., and started preparing for battle. However, the Allies were aware of the vessel's presence and began their attack with depth charges. Around 4.35 p.m. the heavily damaged *Ondina* had no choice but to resurface. It was then attacked by four enemy ships and struck by a bomb dropped from an aircraft. Ammunition stored on the submersible's deck exploded, killing some crew members. The Italians managed to sink the ship, but were then taken prisoner. In total, the first mate, two NCOs and three other crew members were killed in the attack.

On July 21st 1942, at 3.17 a.m., *Dandolo* fired four torpedoes at the aircraft carrier *Eagle*, which was transporting aircraft to Malta. The projectiles missed, and the Italian submarine was then attacked by escorting units.

In the first half of July 1942, *Emo* and *Otaria* were patrolling waters south of the Balearic Islands, and were later relieved by *Dandolo* and *Platino*. At the same time *Ascianghi* and *Onice* were patrolling the shores of La Galite. After July 15th the route between La Galite, Cani island, Cape

Bon and Cape Kelibia was patrolled by *Cobalto*, *Dessie* and *Axum*, and later *Malachite*, *Velella*, *Dagabur*, *Bronzo* and *Cobalto*. *Axum* (*tenente di vascello* Renato Ferrini) sighted the minelayer *Welshman*, headed for Malta with supplies, but the vessel wasn't able to get in position for an attack. The eastern areas were patrolled by *Nereide*, *Ondina*, *Perla*, *Asteria* and *Alagi*. Fifteen transports were completed, and 1104.7 tonnes of goods were transported: 800.4 tonnes of petrol, 244.2 tonnes of ammunition, 50.2 tonnes of food and 9.9 tonnes of spare parts.

On August 10th the Italian submarine *Scire* (commanded by Bruno Zelik), distinguished while in service in Alexandria, was sunk off the coast of Haifa. At the time, the vessel was on a similar mission (Operation Gamma). The target was Haifa; the attack was to be conducted by ten divers.

On July 27th, the submersible left La Spezia, and arrived on Leros on August 2nd. On August 6th the vessel left the island, and the attack was planned for the night of August 11th. For the next four days, the vessel took orders from Corvette Captain Max Candiani, the commander of the operation, based on Rhodos. Contact was later lost. The base kept trying to re-establish contact until August 18th, but by then it was obvious that something was wrong. On August 31st, it was officially announced that the ship had been lost while on a mission.

The British intelligence were able to intercept communications regarding the planned operation thanks to Enigma. The waters in the vicinity of Haifa were well secured, preventing *Scire* from retreating. At 10.30 a.m., an airplane was sighted, and the vessel was soon attacked with depth charges by *Islay*, an anti-submarine trawler. The heavily damaged *Scire* resurfaced to save her crew, but this meant getting under fire from the coastal artillery. The sail and the bow of the vessel were struck, and the vessel sank quickly before anyone could leave it. *Islay* then approached the point where *Scire* disappeared into the ocean and dropped a further six depth charges. On August 14th, the remains of two participants of Gamma were discovered on the shores, which suggests that some sailors made it out of the ship alive and were then killed by the last bombs. The ship's crew perished with her: the captain, six other officers, 42 NCOs and mates, and eleven commandos from the Decima Flottiglia MAS.

Break the pedestal!

The famous *Pedestal* convoy faced danger from the Italian fleet as well as 21 German and Italian submarines, all gathered in the Strait of Sicily. Seven Italian *sommergibili* were placed between the Balearic Islands and Algiers, among them *Dagabur* and *Uarsciek*, and north of Tunisia (Tunis) and in the vicinity of Cape Bon, a further twelve, among them *Alagi*, *Ascianghi*, *Axum* and *Dessiè*.

In the early morning of August 11th, the convoy was attacked by *Volframio* and *Uarsciek*. On August 7th, *Volframio* was sent to the area between Algeria, Ibiza and Majorca (longitude 1°40' E to 2°40' E). *Uarsciek* was also patrolling this area, and at 4.38 a.m. it sighted the convoy. It shot three torpedoes at the aircraft carrier *Furious*. The Italians reported two hits, but this was unconfirmed by the British. For the next few hours, *Uarsciek* was under attack with depth charges. It only managed to resurface and report the sighting of the

Acciaio shortly after entering service, January 1942 [Photo *Storia Militare Dossier No. 11*]

Emo in the Suda Strait, Crete, January 5, 1942. A tug boat is helping it navigate the waters. *Emo* had just successfully completed a transport mission to Bardi, Libya, earlier returning to the Mediterranean Sea after staying for a while in the Atlantic *sommergibili* base in Bordeaux. In the background, the anchored torpedo ship *Cassipea* can be seen [Photo *Storia Militare Dossier No. 11*]

***Ammiraglio Millo* leaving the Mar Piccolo Strait in Toranto to deliver an urgent load of 155 tonnes of ammunition to Tripolis, January 26th 1942 [Photo *Storia Militare Dossier No. 11*]**

***Pietro Micca* manoeuvreing in the Mar Piccolo Strait in Toranto, January 30, 1942. The vessel had just returned from a transport mission to Tripolis, during which it delivered 156.4 tonnes of cargo [Photo *Storia Militare Dossier No. 11*]**

The 102/35 gun and the conning tower of *Squalo*, probably Trapani, late January 1942 [Photo *Storia Militare Dossier No. 2*]

Pedestal operation ships at 9.30. On August 13th *Uarsciek* was attacked by aircraft, damaged and forced to return to base.

In the night of August 12th, the destroyer *Wolverine*'s radar detected an unidentified submarine in close proximity. The vessel ploughed forwards at 26 knots, ramming and sinking the Italian submersible *Dagabur* (*tenente di vascello* Renoto Pecori). The entire crew perished. *Wolverine* sustained heavy damage and barely made it back to Gibraltar. The incident occurred south of the Balearic Islands, around 1 a.m. The vessel left Cagliari and entered the area patrolled by *Uarsciek*. On August 11th, south of the Balearic Islands, *Dagabur* encountered *Furious*, escorted by eight destroyers. The Italians attempted to get into a good attack position on the surface, but were rammed and sank; their position was 37°18' N, 1°58' E. Pecori, five other officers and 39 NCOs and sailors perished.

On August 12th, the submarine *Cobalto* was lost. The *sommergibible* had only entered service five months earlier, on March 18th 1942. Her base of operations was Augusta and at the time had only completed one patrol. On July 30th, it was patrolling the waters near La Galite, but no enemy forces were encountered. On August 11th or August 12th, the ship left her base again, commanded by *tenente di vascello* Raffaele Amicarelli. *Cobalto* was supposed to intercept the *Pedestal* convoy as well. Her planned operational area were the waters off the northern coast of Tunisia. At 1.45 p.m., the vessel was 30 miles north of La Galite. A group of twelve destroyers was then sighted, between 12 and 18 kilometres away. The vessel dove to around fifty meters and attempted to get into an attack position, surfacing to periscope depth to confirm its position via periscope two or three times. Around 2 p.m. the ship was ready to fire torpedoes at the enemy, resurfaced to periscope depth and started turning north, when an enemy destroyer was sighted just three hundred meters away. In fact, the first bombs were dropped by the destroyers HMS *Ithuriel* and *Pathfinder*. *Cobalto* was at 18 meters at the time; its sail and controls were damaged. The crew hastily dove to 120 meters. The British then dropped more depth charges. The bombs damaged the right engine and destroyed the radio system. Despite the crew's efforts, the vessel started resurfacing. To make matters worse, the trapdoors were damaged in the explosion and the crew was unable to open them. After several frantic attempts, the main trapdoor and front trapdoors were finally opened. The crew attempted to get out a gun onto the deck and defend the ship. *Ituriel*, at the time around 300-350 meters away from *Cobalto*, opened cannon and machine gun fire. One of the projectiles ripped a large hole in the sail. The destroyer then attempted to ram the submarine. The captain of the *sommergibile* ordered to sink and abandon ship. Soon afterwards the vessels collided; the stern section was mostly submerged at that point, but the bow was still above the water line. It was then that the destroyer struck the submarine in the starboard side, right above the sail. The hull of *Ithuriel* lodged itself quite firmly in the submarine; this gave three Italian sailors the opportunity to escape on-board the British vessel; in turn, four British crewmembers jumped down onto the sinking submarine. At 5.02 p.m. the Italian vessel disappeared from the surface. Everyone in the Italian crew was taken prisoner by the *Ithuriel*. Two Italians perished in the fight: *sottotenente di vascello* Giovanni Gardella and sailor Mario Volpe. Two British sailors were also killed in the risky attempt to intercept *Cobalto*. The bow of the destroyer was heavily damaged by the accident, forcing the ship to return to Gibraltar.

On August 12th, the convoy reached the most dangerous point in its journey – the Strait of Sicily.

At 7 p.m., group *Z* fell back, as planned. Merchant ships, twelve destroyers and four cruisers proceeded onwards. The convoy was now comprised of two columns instead of four. The commander was now rear admiral Burroughs, sailing on the light cruiser *Nigeria*. After just an hour the vessel was torpedoed by *Axum* and was forced to head back to Gibraltar.

The first *sommergibile* to attack (at 18.55) was *Dessiè* (*tenente di vascello* Renato Scandola). In a short time, eight torpedoes were fired at the steam ship *Brisbane Star* (12 971 BRT), heavily damaging it. The vessel was initially immobilized, but ultimately made it back to Malta. On the way there, it was attacked again by German torpedo bombers. The Italian vessel was attacked by the escorting destroyers. In 90 minutes, 120 depth charges were dropped, but none of them caused any significant damage. On August 13th, *Dessiè* was attacked by the escorting vessels again, with heavy casualties. Heavily damaged, it managed to return to Italy. The sinking of the British cargo ship *Deucalion* (7516 BRT) is also attributed to *Dessiè*, but it was actually sunk by He 111 torpedo bombers.

At 7.27 p.m. *tenente di vascello* Renato Ferrini, the commander of *Axum*, raised the periscope. It was already dark outside. Ferrini started manoeuvring to get into a satisfactory position. Fifteen minutes later, when he looked through the periscope again, he saw two vessels and a merchant ship directly ahead, around 1300-1800 meters away. All this took place north of Bizerta. At 7.55 p.m. Ferrini fired four torpedoes; after 63 seconds an explosion was heard, and a further two after 27 seconds. *Axum*'s torpedoes hit the cruiser *Nigeria* (8530 tonnes). She was struck in the port side, below the foremast. The torpedo ripped a hole more than ten meters long; the front (bow?) boiler room and many other rooms were flooded. The vessel developed a list and lost propulsion for fifteen minutes. With 52 dead and many wounded, three destroyers escorted her back to Gibraltar; she didn't sail again until September 1943. The light (anti-aircraft) cruiser *Cairo* (4190 tonnes) was struck by two torpedoes in her stern section, started taking in water, caught on fire and was unable to move, with the crew escaping. The vessel was sunk by the destroyer *Pathfinder*; this decision was made because towing her would weaken the convoy. 23 or 24 sailors perished; the rest were evacuated. The last victim was the tanker *Ohio* (9614 tonnes): she was struck in the centre hull section and caught fire. The crew managed to contain the fire and resume their journey. Her captain, 39 year old Dudley Mason, upon seeing the two torpedoes striking his vessel only managed to say 'Hold on! If there's a third one...', before an enormous, eight meter wide hole was ripped in the hull of his tanker.

Alagi in the port of Pola, early 1942 [Photo *Storia Militare Dossier No. 11*]

The attack caused a massive confusion. The cargo ship *Empire Hope* was forced to abruptly change course to avoid hitting the burning *Ohio*. With the columns broken, the ships strived to avoid hitting each other. Five minutes after the attack *Axum* found itself in a difficult situation, being attacked by depth charges. The Italians dove to 100 meters and turned their engines off; the attack lasted two hours. At 10.30 p.m., with the enemy losing interest in destroying the submarine, the crew resurfaced again and saw three burning silhouettes and two destroyers using light

Porfido during an exercise nearby Pola, early 1942 [Photo *Storia Militare Dossier No. 11*]

February 22nd, Toranto, *Argento* ready to be launched in the Tosi shipyard [Photo *Storia Militare Dossier No. 11*]

signals to communicate. *Asum* dove again rapidly and managed to avoid pursuit. From that point onwards, it easy to predict the route taken by the convoy: it had to navigate between the shores of Tunisia, shallows and minefields.

Taking advantage of the situation, the Italian submarine *Alagi* (*tenente di vascello* Sergio Puccini), located at 37°28'N 10°38'E at the time (around 1800 meters away), fired a full burst of torpedoes at 9.05 p.m. One of the torpedoes struck the cruiser *Kenya* (8500 tonnes, at 9.12 p.m.) and exploded on the starboard side, close to the stern. The vessel did not sink, but three of her crew were killed. *Kenya* later underwent repairs that lasted until December. The second torpedo passed under the hull of the cruiser. Another two torpedoes from the blast struck the British cargo ship *Clan Feruson* (7347 BRT); the ship fell apart in the resulting explosion, having been heavily damaged by German aircraft beforehand.

At dusk (around 9 p.m.) the convoy came under attack from enemy aircraft again: Ju 88 and Italian Savoi. The Axis planes were flying low to drop torpedoes on the scattered convoy. *Empire Hope* (12 688 BRT) was heavily damaged as the bombs struck its hold and caused the aviation fuel inside to explode in a great blast. *Empire Hope* was now in flames and only just moving. The ship was deemed lost; her crew was rescued by HMS *Penn*. Later, at 11.45 p.m., the vessel was struck by another torpedo fired by *sommergibile Brozno*, (*tenente di vascello* Cesare Buldrini), a few miles away from the site of previous attacks. The wreck stayed afloat and was eventually sunk by the destroyer HMS *Bramham*, near La Goletta in Tunisia.

Just before the dawn of August 14th the resurfaced *Granito* (*tenente di vascello* Leo Sposito) sighted *Force X* vessels, returning to Gibraltar. Ship 6 was sent east of La Galite. The convoy's ships were sighted, but no possibility of attack arose. At 4.47 a.m. the first three vessels could be seen zigzagging. The two closest units were around four kilometres away at that point. The Italians closed the distance to around a half of that and opened fire at 4.51 a.m. Four destroyers were also identified on the starboard side. At 4.52 a.m. and 4.53 a.m. *Granito* fired four further torpedoes at the slightly damaged light cruiser *Kenya* and her escorting destroyer. In total, five torpedoes were fired. The *sommergibile* then dove hastily, because headed her way were two other vessels, clearly intending to ram the submarine. In actuality, one of those units was *Kenya*. A minute later, the Italians heard two explosions and assumed they had hit the second target. That target was the destroyer *Ashanti*, which was now counter-attacking with depth charges. At 5.50 a.m., it resurfaced and reported the incident, and at 6.10 a.m. it dove quickly again after an aircraft was sighted, although it was probably a Luftwaffe reconnaissance unit.

At the beginning of August 1943, *Axum*, *Velella* and *Granito* were located south of La Galite.

Tritone is being completed in the Monfalcone shipyard, spring of 1942 [Photo *Storia Militare Dossier No. 11*]

Starting on August 3rd, more *sommergibili* were sent to the western areas. *Giada*, *Dagabur*, *Uarsciek* and *Volframio* were all operating on Algerian waters. The other vessels were placed on the predictable points of the route of the convoy, which was headed for Malta, namely: *Ascianghi*, *Axum*, *Alagi*, *Bronzo* and *Dessiè* in *Zona A*, *Avorio*, *Cobalto* and *Granito* in *Zona B*, and *Emo*, *Dandolo* and *Ontaria* in *Zona C*. In the second half of the month *Porfido* appeared on the waters close to Valencia, but had no significant victories. *Bandiera*, *Manotti*, *Pisani*, *Sqalo* and *H2* were patrolling metropolitan waters. Eleven transports totalling 710.8 tonnes of goods were also completed in this month.

The hunt for *sommergibili*

At 4.20 p.m. on September 14th 1942 *Alabastro* (*tenente di vascello* Giovanni Bonadies) was sunk north of Bougie by *Sunderland* of the 202nd RAF Squadron. The vessel departed Cagliari a day earlier and embarked on its first combat mission. The Italians only realized that the vessel was sunk resurfaced after the war. The commander, four

Flutto underoing sea trials on the Upper Adriatic, March 1942. Two Carley lifeboats can be seen in front of the cannon base [Photo *Storia Militare Dossier No. 11*]

other officers and 39 NCOs and sailors perished in the attack.

In September 1942 eighteen *sommergibili* carried out 21 missions. *Velella* and *Asteria* were patrolling the area around the Balearic Islands at the beginning of the month, while *Argo* and *Alabatro* were operating along the northern coast of Africa, later to be relieved by *Argento* and *Nichelio*. In the middle of the month *Sirena* was patrolling waters east of Rhodos. Starting on September 24th, *Ametista* and *Nereide* patrolled the areas south of Crete. Type *H* vessels patrolled territorial waters twice. *Atropo*, *Zoea*, *Bragadin*, *Narvallo* and *Santarosa* completed eight transports for the African front.

In October 1942 *Argento*, *Niechelio*, *Mocenigo*, *Dandolo*, *Emo* and *Brin* were patrolling close to the Balearic Islands. Because of *Furious*'s planned mission, additional units were sent to the area: *Corallo*, *Turchese*, *Topazio* and *Axum*. At the end of the month *Porfido*, *Nichelio*, *Asteria* and *Argo* were sent to hunt the enemy around La Galite. Ten transports were attempted, eight of which were completed successfully: five *sommergibili* delivered 570.4 tonnes of goods to Africa.

At the beginning of November *sommergibile Granito* (*terente di vascello* Leo Sposito) brought 22.4 tons of ammunition to Africa. On November 5th, she reached Tubruq, and after unloading, returned to her Augusta base on November 8th. She departed again on the same day, crossed the Strait of Messina and headed for Algerian shores, where she was to join other vessels in countering Operation Torch. The last report from *Granito* was on 10.15 a.m. the next day. On November 9th 1942 the British submarine *Saracen* torpedoed and sank that *sommergibile*. The attack happened close to Trapani (northwest of Cape San Vito). The Italian ship was on the surface. At 3.44 p.m. *Saracen* fired four torpedoes from a distance of 730 meters, three of which struck the target. *Granito* sank at 38°34' N 12°09' E; her entire crew perished: the commander, four officers and 42 NCOs and sailors.

The Italians sustained further casualties in November. *Antonio Sciesa* was sunk by USAF aircraft. On November 3rd the vessel left Tarent and headed for Tubruq, reaching it three days later. While the ship was being unloaded on the same day, around 4 p.m., three bombs dropped from enemy aircraft struck the *Antonio*. Five officers and eighteen NCOs and sailors perished, and the vessel sank to the bottom of the base. On November 12th, with the Allies getting closer, the wreck was raised and destroyed in an explosion. In her life the ship completed six transport missions, delivering 369.5 tonnes of cargo.

Emo (*tenente di vascello* Giuseppe Franco) was attacked on Algerian waters on November 10th,

Avorio leaving Cagliari, March 24 1942 [Photo *Storia Militare Dossier No. 11*]

SLC containers can be seen on the deck of *Ambra*, La Spezia, April 1942 [Photo *Storia Militare Dossier No. 11*]

while fully submerged, by the anti-submarine trawler *Lord Nuffield*. On November 7th *Emo* left Cagliari and headed to its designated hunting zone south of Sardinia, then north of Algeria. It was there that *Emo* met her demise. Heavily damaged by depth charges, it was forced to resurface. A brief, but intense artillery battle ensued, in which fourteen of *Emo*'s crew were killed. Franco was unable to escape since the engines were damaged, so he ordered the crew to sink the vessel. Survivors were then taken prisoner by the British.

On November 8th, two submerged submarines collided close to Cape Bougaroni. The vessels involved were *Diaspro* and *Alagi*. Both were in the

Port of Cagliari, probably April 16, 1942. *Venioro* is returning from its penultimate mission. The vessel was patrolling waters south of the Balearic Islands [Photo *Storia Militare Dossier No. 2*]

Argo in the port of *Cagliari*, May 1942 (Photo *Storia Militare Dossier No. 11*)

process of taking position in their hunt zones. *Diaspro*'s damages weren't significant, but *Alagi*'s kiosk was heavily damaged and had to return to Naples. By December, the vessel was back on the sea.

Quench the Torch

The *sommergibili* had their small successes in trying to fight against the landing of allied forces in the French colonial land properties (operation *Torch*).

On 12 November, at night *Argento*, *Diaspro* and *Argo* carried out offensive patrols in the Bougie region. Argo (*tenente di vascello* Pasquale Gigli) slipped into the roadstead of the port. Gigli rested the ship at the bottom of the sea and for two hours, he saw through the periscope two Corvettes circulating. When the situation calmed down, the *sommergibile* started to attack. At 5.57, *Argo* fired two double torpedoes towards the vessels which berthed in the port. In the attack, the Italians sunk the English auxiliary unit aircraft defence *Tynwald* (2.376 t) and destroyed the transport ship *Awatera* (2.376 t) which had already been bomb-damaged by the air force.

On November 15, 1942, at 3.45 a.m., near Bougie, *Ascianghi* (*tenente di vascello* Rino Erler) torpedoed and sank the fast HMS Algerine (1,040 t) minesweeper. Battleship 11 sailed to the Algerian seas. In the night of November 15, it entered the roadstead of the port and then spotted the enemy vessels as they were leaving the port. Erler mistakenly identified the group as a cruiser escorted by two gunboats. As she floated on the surface of the water, at 3.39 a.m., she fired two torpedoes towards the second vessel in the line. The second pair of torpedoes was fired towards the last ship of the formation, and those were well-aimed. The attacked ship quickly disappeared under water, it was 5 nm to the North off the Carbon Cape. Twenty-four out of the 56 crew members of the minesweeper were killed. The *Ascianghi* managed to escape the chase, and on the next day, she turned back to their hunting zone. On 18 November, she safely returned to Naples.

Benito Mussolini visiting the submarine base in Cagliari, *Argo* visible in the background, May 14 1942 [Photo *Storia Militare Dossier No. 2*]

On 28 November, 1942, *Dessiè* (*tenente di vascello* Alberto Gorini) was sighted somewhere north off Annaby, 10 nm off the Bon Cape, belonging to the 500 Squadron RAF *Hudson*. Soon the Italian ship was attacked with depth bombs by the Canadian gunboats HMCS *Quentin* and *Quiberon*. He emerged for a moment, but at 14.05 p.m., she rested on the seabed. The entire crew was killed: the Commander, four other officers and 43 non-commissioned officers and mariners. On 18 November, the ship left Messina. At 19.12 p.m. on 27 November, she sent her last message.

November of 1942 was a busy month for the Italian submarine, which was obviously related to what was happening on the northern coast of Africa. From 7 November, *Axum* and *Topazio* took their positions in the area of the Caxine Cape, and *Bronzo*, *Nichelio* and *Argo* lurked near Bizerte. The Algerian seas were divided into two zones: Zona A and B, and on November 8, the sea was full of *sommergibili*. *Avorio*, *Alagi*, *Corallo*, *Diaspro* and *Turchese* arrived in Zona A, and *Aradam*, *Acciaio*, *Argento*, *Asteria*, *Brin*, *Dandolo*, *Emo*, *Mocenigo*, *Porfido*, *Platino* and *Velella* in Zona B. Until 14 November, *Ascianghi*, *Volframio*, *Giada* and *Galatea* joined the rest of the ships. From 18 November, some ships began to leave those zones. By 20 November, the above mentioned ships had replaced *Dessiè*, *Malachite*, *Dandolo*, *Nichelio*, *Asteria* and *Giada*, and the last two units went on a patrol for the second time that month. In the eastern part of the sea, only *Sirena*, *Beilul* and *Onice* operated, and they had their base in Leros. The upper Adriatic Sea was patrolled by *Bandiera* and by *Squalo*. In addition, in 17 transport missions to North Africa, the 955.9 t of goods and petrol were supplied and picked up at the place of destination. Between 13 November, 1942, and 6 January, 1943, *Delfino* provided the African troops with 200 tons of ammunition and fuel. The ship's crew managed to knock down *Sunderland*. *Micca* was responsible for similar tasks, as she transported 2163 tons of supplies to the army front.

The success of the Amber and x^a mas

On 6 December 1942, the Italian submarine Profido (*tenente di vascello* Giovanni Lorenzotti) was sunk in the sea around La Galite. The British equivalent of *Tigris* was her conqueror. On the evening of 2 December, *sommergibile* left Cagliari, and her job was to set traps in the area of the Bone port. At 1.50 a.m., on 6 December, *Porfido* started to emerge and was spotted by British *Tigris*. The British were the first to fire their torpedoes. They managed to pass by the first one, but the second one hit the engine room. The ship sank in 20 seconds at position 38°10'N and 8°35'E, about 90 nm north off Bone. The Commander, five other mariners and 38 non-commissioned officers and mariners were killed. *Tigris* pulled out four survivors from the water.

Between December 4 and 15, *Amber* (*tenente di vascello* Mario Arillo) operated as the troop transport for S.L.C.[8] and for the diver assault. The N.A. 1 Operation began formally on December 1. On board the ship, there were three S.L.C. with six people that were their crews and 10 Gamma people (five from the army and the same number from the Navy, they were commanded by *tenente del Corpo delle armi navali* Agostino Morello). On December 4, in the early afternoon, the ship departed La Spezia, and three days later she reached the Algerian waters. The weather conditions were adverse, so they waited to start the operation until 11 a.m. Navigating a partially immersed vessel turned out to be difficult; *Ambra* among others heavily hit the seabed at a depth of 90 m. Finally, they managed to sneak into the roadstead, where they saw around six merchant ships berthed. Between 10.30 and 11.00 at night, the divers left *Amber*` deck and within the next 20 minutes, the *maile* did the same. The original plan failed, and as a result, the attack was carried out by one manned torpedo and five divers. The rest of the attackers returned to find the sommergibile. Soon alarm was raised, as one of the divers had been captured by the enemy. Despite the risk,

Volframio cruising in the summer of 1942. A 100/47 OTO model 1938 cannon can be seen in the foreground, and above two twin-barrelled Breda model 31 da 13.2mm machine guns can be seen on the conning tower. The person to the left of the guns was the ship's commander at the time – tenente di vascello Giovanni Manunta [Photo *Storia Militare Dossier No. 11*]

Monfalcone, early summer of 1942. *Porfido* in the CRDA shipyard, where it was built, and where it entered service in January 1942. It would soon depart for Cagliari and commence its short military career, which will be ended later in December by its British equivalent, HMS *Tigris* [Photo *Storia Militare Dossier No. 3*]

Beirut, July 1942, *sommergibile Perla* photographed a few days after capture [Photo *Storia Militare Dossier No. 3*]

the ship remained in the neighbouring seas until 2.54 a.m., as the crew was waiting for the commandos to return from the Mission. However, all of them were eventually captured. During the retreat, *Ambra* hit some wreck, fortunately without consequences. On 12 December at 19:45 p.m., the ship came up to the surface, for the first time after 36 hours had passed. At noon on December 15, the *sommergibile* returned to Spezia. Because of the action, the ocean steamers *Vanquisher* (7.174 BRT) and *Berto* (1.493 BRT) were sunk and the merchant ships *Empire Centaur* (7.041 BRT) and *Armattan* (4.558 GRT) were damaged. The Commander of *Amber* was given the *Medaglia d'Oro al Valor Militare* in reward for that action, and 12 commandos were awarded the Medaglia d'Argento al Valor Militare, and next Commandor received *the Croce di guerra al valor militarne.*

On 13 December, 1942, near Bougie, Corallo (*tenente di vascello* Guido Guidi) was lost. He left Cagliari on 10 December and headed for her designated sector between Bizerta and Bone. No message was sent by that *sommergibile* ever after and they kept trying to contact the vessel until 23 December.

In the night of the unlucky day, *Corallo* came across four English frigates. This happened about 40 nm off Bougie. The course of the accident is not

British steam ship *Empire Hope* (12 688 BRT). Sunk by *Bronzo* on August 12, 1942 in the Strait of Sicily [Photo *Storia Militare Dossier No. 11*]

clear; the warship was going to be hit by the opponent's heavy gun when she tried to submerge, or he was flushed out by depth bombs. It is certain, however, that her fate was sealed by the battering ram of the frigate[10] *Enchantress*, which as a result was also seriously damaged. The Italian warship sank with all its crew in the position of 36°58'N and 5°07'E. The list of victims included the Commander, five other officers and 43 non-commissioned officers and seamen.

On 14 December, 1942, at about 5.56 a.m., near Bone, *Mocenigo* (*tenente di vascello* Alberto Longhi) severely damaged the light anti-aircraft cruiser *HMS Argonaut*. The Italians fired four torpedoes against the unit that was dominating the group of ships identified as the Tribal class of destroyers.

However, *Argonaut* turned out to be the goal, and was hit in the bow and stern by two torpedoes. Three people were killed on board the warship. The cruise ship returned to service a year later.

The massacre at Uarsciek

On 14 December, 1942, the British Destroyer *Petard* and Greek *Vasilissa Olga* detected and attacked the *sommergibile Uarsciek* (*tenente di vascello* Gaetano Arezzo della Targia) located South-East off Malta. On December 11, the unit left Augusta and headed 50 nm south of Malta. The gunboats involved in the loss of the *sommergibile* followed from Bengasi to Malta.

The Italians also had been spotted by Allied ships, which was at about 04.05 a.m., in the posi-

Anti-aircraft cruiser *Cairo*, sunk by Axum in the Strait of Sicily on August 12 1942 [Photo *Storia Militare Dossier No. 11*]

Another victim of *sommergibili* hunt organized on August 12, light cruiser *Nigeria* damaged by a torpedo fired from *Axum* [Photo *Storia Militare Dossier No. 11*]

tion of 35°08'N and 14°22'E. The object spotted by the destroyers was 3000 m away from them. In this dark and moonless night, it was considered initially to be a surface vessel heading in the same direction. Once discovered that it was an underwater vessel, *Petard* tried to contact her using the aldis lamp, remembering that their own P-35 was supposed to be in the vicinity. The Italians answered by launching two torpedoes from their torpedo tubes. The attack was carried out on the surface, however, immediately after that, the Italians submerged. Two loud explosions were heard, yet no hit was confirmed. *Petard* returned towards the torpedoes, thus reducing their silhouette and informed the Greeks about the danger.

The asdic *Vasilissa Olga* immediately received a message. A moment later, *Petarda*, thanks to the data received, fired the first bombs. After the explosion, contact was lost; however, *Petarda* carried out another attack, trusting his intuition. The Greeks did the same, a moment later. Underwater monitoring of the destroyers reported the sound of removing water form ballast tanks. Soon in the right frontal quarter of *Petarda*, in a distance of approximately 200 m, the Italians appeared. During the quick submersion maneuver, they made a mistake, resulting in *Uarsciek* going 160 m down the water, double exceeding the norm. Returning to a lower depth was also difficult, and the conning tower of the vessel jumped out of the water for a while. There was no time to descent to sufficient depth, as the gunboats were already deploying depth charges. *Uarsciek* was heavily damaged, water was leaking into the ship. The ship was eventually forced to come up to the surface.

The crew wanted to start an artillery attach and in the meantime start the scuttling procedure. Headlights illuminated the Italian ship. The opponent knew what was going to happen, and in order to avoid scuttling, both destroyers immediately cannonaded *Uarsciek* with their small-calibre and machine guns. Even though they were mainly shooting at the crew, who hid under the ship deck in the attempt to survive, , the procedure was commenced.

The Commander, the Deputy Commander of *sottotenente di vascello* Remigio Dapiran and 16 non-commissioned officers and seamen were killed in the massacre. Many Italians were injured.

The affair of the massacre remains unclear. At one point, the *Petarda* shooters stopped fire, so they must have been horrified by that bloody inci-

Volframio submerged, probably taken in the summer of 1942 [Photo *Storia Militare Dossier No. 11*]

Granito photographed probably on waters near Calgiari, autumn of 1942 (Photo *Storia Militare Dossier No. 11*)

Gorgo entering service, November 1942 [Photo *Storia Militare Dossier No. 11*]

dent. They also did not react to the orders to resume fire. The defenceless Italians gathered at the stern of their ship. Then suddenly they received a series from the machine gun on the bridge of the British ship, and some of the Italians were killed. It is not unclear who fired those shots, yet the fact is that the Commander of *Petarda* did not notice that sommergibile was on a collision course. The destroyer struck with the beak just behind the kiosk, and a moment later it withdrew and slipped off the hull of the Italian ship, all that accompanied by a rumour of sheet metal tearing apart.

Another version of this event is presented by *Petarda's* physician, William Prendergast and by the survivors. According to them, initially only Arezzo della Targia and Dapirana were killed, and the massacre started as the Commander of *Petarda*, lieutenant commander Mark Thornton, who had already seen sommergibile as their booty, feared that the Italians might yet be able to sink

Anti-aircraft tender HMS *Tynwald*, sunk on November 12 by *Argo*. In the second picture: another victim of that *sommergibile*, troopship *Awatea* (13 482 BRT) [Photo *Storia Militare Dossier No. 11*]

Ruggiero Settimo on the left, and *Otaria* anchored in Toranto in December 1942 [Photo *Storia Militare Dossier No. 11*]

it. He was to take a machine gun and open fire on the people in the water. He ordered the same to his subordinates, yet they did it reluctantly, after the commander repeated the order. After returning to the base and once the doctor's report was presented, Thornton was degraded and ordered to sit behind the desk.

The scuttling procedure failed. The boarding party made of seven men from *Petarda* led by naval cadet Peter A.T. Goddard, took over the ship and has found numerous documents. The Commander's body lied on the kiosk, and next to him they placed a bag full of secret maps, codes etc. The Italians themselves claim that they had thrown overboard the secret documents, ciphers and the encryption machine.

Thirty survivors[11] from the submarine were taken out of the water only after several hours. Many of them were injured; some severely wounded. The chief engineer was to be called to go under the deck of the *sommergibile*, to turn off the devices and to indicate that all the valves were closed and to make sure the detonators of self-destructive system were inactive. He remained on *Uarsciek* while it was being towed. At dawn, they took away the dead bodies of the Italians, and the towing device was fixed too. Then the two Italian fighters flew over the sailing ships, they probably recognized them as their own, as they failed to take any action. At 11 a.m., the boarding party evacuated, and at 11.33 a.m. the tow broke off for the second time. The ship sank. The Royal Navy flag was the last to disappear underwater (it was hung on *Uarsciek* in the meantime).

In December 1942, 33 the *sommergibili* carried out 44 missions. At the beginning of the month, *Nichelio*, *Asteria*, and *Giada* patrolled the area between the Bougaroni Cape and the island of La Galite. Later on, they had been replaced by *Alagi*, *Bronzo*, *Galatea*, *Porfido* and *Volframio*, which

Cagliari, December 4, 1942, damage to *Asteria's* conning tower visible. While patrolling Algierian waters, it collided with the hull of an enemy ship. It was then attacked with depth charges, damaged and forced to return to base [Photo *Storia Militare Dossier No. 11*]

The scuttling of *Uarsciek*, December 15, 1942. The British managed to prevent the vessel from sinking, but were unable to tow it to Malta [Photo *Storia Militare Dossier No. 11*]

Light cruiser HMS *Argonaut*. On December 14, it was heavily damaged by *Moeceni* [Photo *Storia Militare Dossier No. 11*]

Another shot of *Uarsciek*, taken from the deck of an enemy vessel [Photo *Storia Militare Dossier No. 3*]

took up their positions in the area of Ajaccio, when the Italian army occupied Corsica. Between 11 and 16 of December the ships sailing on the Algerian seas had been withdrawn and replaced by *Argento*, *Corallo*, *Mocenigo*, *Diaspro* and *Malachite*. Somewhere in the mid of the month, the *sommergibili* named *Topazio* and *Uarsciek* returned to the waters surrounding Malta. They tried to disturb the activity of the Force K, the ships which menaced the shipping transport between Italy and Libya. *Nereide*, *Ametista*, *Galatea* and *Aradam* operated in the central-eastern part of the archipelago. 590 t of materials were supplied to North Africa in 10 transport missions.

In the second half of 1942, the *sommergibili* transported 4561.3 tons of supplies in 71 missions. Over the year, 80 missions were carried out, out of which 78 were completed successfully (70% more than in the previous year), when 5295.1 t of supplies were transported (27% more than in the previous year, mainly because smaller vessels were used in the operation). In July, 15 missions were carried out, which transported 1104.7 tons of materials, and in November, 17 missions in which more than 950 tonnes of fuel and materials were transported.

1942, the Italian submarines transported 733,8 tons of supplies in nine missions.

Endnotes

1 Another source claims that the ship was hit in the starboard.
2 Or south-east.
3 According to other sources, along with Amato died two more officers and 52 petty officers and seamen.
4 Some sources also mention the 204. Squadron.
5 He received his second Distinguished Flying Cross for that attempt.
6 The crew could have been a little bigger – 49 members.
7 Other sources claim that the ship was going to attack two battleships or was twice in a position to sink the aircraft carrier *Indomitable*.
8 Manned torpedoes.
9 Some sources give the name *Harmattan*.
10 Possibly a gunboat.
11 Some sources report 32 survivors.

Scirè port side. Version before August 1940

Drawings: **Carlo Cestra**

Starboard side

Scirè port side. Version after September 1940. To camouflage the Scirè, the silhouette of a fishing boat with the bow in the direction opposite to that of the submarine was painted on the sides of the hull

Drawings: **Carlo Cestra**

starboard side

The road to fighter pilot at sea

Frank van der Avoort, Johan Franken

For three days the authors of this article had been a guest aboard the aircraft carrier USS Dwight D. Eisenhower while patrolling off the coast of Pakistan in service of operations in Afghanistan. On board the 5,500 people all do their job with the primary purpose to let the key players off the ship fly their aircraft. Former instructor pilot and today's Squadron Commander "Flea", sets out for us how the road to a carrier fighter pilot looks.

Flight School

To become a pilot in the U.S. Navy, the first training for everyone starts at the U.S. Naval Academy in Annapolis. When finished, the trainee pilot reports at "The Cradle of Naval Aviation", NAS Pensacola. Here is determined in about 25 hours whether the student has sufficient construction to fly. Here is also situated the adjacent "Ground School" in which the student learns the basic principles of aerodynamics, avionics, navigation and meteorology.

The next step is the Primary Flight Training on the T-34 Turbo Mentor. Depending on the results of these 22 weeks the pilot training continues as helicopter pilot, multi-engine pilot or "Tail Hooker" flying from an aircraft carrier

The Tail Hookers continue to NAS Kingsville or NAS Meridian to train on the T-45 Goshawk. Here one learns to fly in about 27 weeks on this of the

A picture of the control-tower during the last recovery of the day

This Superhornet finds his way in the sky towards Afghanistan after his catapult start

A landing F(A)-18 at the point it catches the wire

BAE Hawk derived jet trainer. Addressed issues are Basic Instrument Flying, Formation, Night Flying and Navigation. In the second part of the Goshawk training in another 23 weeks the basic principles of Bombing, Air Combat Maneuvering, Advanced Instruments, Low-level navigation, Formation flying and Carrier Qualification are learned.

Carrier Qualification

Especially the Carrier Qualification is an important part of the course. Pilots practice landings on a simulated flight deck that is part of a normal runway on a normal airfield. This Field Carrier Landing Practices (FLCP) makes the pilot familiar with the small size of the flight deck but also with the Meat Ball. The latter is a system of lights, lenses and mirrors which will guide the pilot for the last ¾ mile of the approach to see whether he is too high, too low or just at the right height. The pilot makes a total of 100 touch-and-go's with the tail hook of the T-45 retracted. There are no arresting brake cables at this runway to stop the aircraft as it happens at a real aircraft carrier. Another ad-

Everyday a Hawkeye radar plane will be launced first followed by the strike-package

The deckcrew a busy to prepare the next launch on the tiny flightdeck

vantage of the touch-and-go's is that an average of 10 landing exercises with different fuel levels can be made in a single flight. The FLCP missions are flown during both day and night.

After FLCP the student flies with his T-45 Goshawk for the first time to a real carrier at sea. Sqn. Com Flea states, "Of the nerves I had hardly slept the night before but at the sight of the carrier with its foaming wake in the blue green sea, I knew immediately that this was one of the best experiences of my life." During the first part of the approach the pilot is constantly assisted by the instructions of the Landing Signal Officers (LSO). These are themselves experienced pilots situated at the actual touch-down position at the flight deck. With the help of various modern and less modern communication instruments the LSO's talk the pilot exactly to the right approach

Almost every communication on the flightdeck is done by hand signals

heading. It takes some practice during the nerve breaking approach to listen and respond to the information through the radio. Yet the pilot flies the approach to the carrier almost entirely on the spoken instructions. Only the last ¾ mile of the approach is flown visually. The pilot focuses his attention entirely on the old but highly reliable optical landing system of lenses and mirrors.

The landing itself is also called a controlled crash. Once approached the carrier at only a few meters, the pilot is applying full throttle to have enough power to make a possible re-launch if it misses one of the four stretched cables. The best cables to "grab" is cable 2 or 3. If one takes the first cable, the plane was too low. The fourth cable was actually too high, so the plane only will stop at the

A view through the eyes of a pilot during the final seconds of the approach

After every flight the recovery at the carrier remains a dangerous task

very end of the flight deck. At any time of the approach the pilot can be ordered by the LSO to apply full power and to abort the landing (Wave Off).

Fleet Replacement Squadron

Now that a T-45 Naval Aviator can land aboard an aircraft carrier it is time to start the training on the F(A)-18 Hornet. This happens with the U.S. Navy at NAS Oceana or NAS Lemoore in the 'Fleet Replacement Squadrons' (FRS). The upcoming F(A)-18 pilots practice their first flights in the safe and relatively inexpensive simulator. Not only the practice of procedures, but even getting used to the flight characteristics of the F(A)-18 is possible in modern simulators. After the flight simulator it's finally time to learn about the brute force of F(A)-18 in real life. The first 4 flights are flown with an instructor pilot in the backseat. Alongside the take-off and landing also flying under VFR and IFR conditions is addressed. The fifth flight is usually the first solo flight where the pilot takes-off and flies a number of predetermined aerobatics maneuvers followed by the landing at the airfield. Through modern means such as the HUD-camera, the instructor evaluates in the debriefing how well the solo pilot performed. Many of the F(A)-18 missions are flown in the dark and therefore immediately after the first solo flight the night flights begins. Formation flying both during day and night is also part of the course. The leading plane is always flown by an instructor and during the first flights there will also always be an instructor pilot in the backseat. Initially only simple 2-ships formations are practiced, but in the end full 4-ships are flown. The first phase of FRS is normally completed after about 15 flights with the practice of the Basic Fighter Maneuvers to make the pilot familiar with the capabilities and limitations of the F(A)-18 Hornet.

With the experience gained at Oceana and Lemoore on the Hornet the pilot leaves in a tem-

The USS Dwight D. Eisenhower with aboard 5.500 persons

The groundcrew accompany the Hornet towards the catapult

Deck crew is facing the heat and blast when this Hornet launches of the deck

All units at the ship have one specially painted commander aircraft like this VFA-131 Wildcats

A colorful Prowler comes in for landing

Superhornet leaves just before sunset

porary Strike Detachment to another airbase. Here one learns in about 10 flights to deploy the F(A)-18 as an instrument in the Air-to-Ground role. They practice the typical pop-up attacks by pulling up and rolling into the target but also the dropping of Laser Guided Bombs (LGB) is practiced. The highlight of this flight consists of firing the 20mm gun and the dropping of some real bombs. Sqn. Com Flea states, "Until that point I only saw the Hornet as a device to fly, but after seeing the tremendous explosions that I had caused, I felt for the first time the power that I held in my hands being an F-18 pilot."

Back to NAS Lemoore or Oceana the pilots learn the basic principles of the Air-to-Air tactics. The use of the radar is an important part. Initially simple 1 versus 1 engagements are practiced, but after some flights this may take up to complex 4 versus 8 situations. Sqn. Com Flea explains, "These flights are not intended for the pilot to become a real Ace but rather to learn about radar interceptions and experience 9G dogfights."

The course at the Fleet Replacement Squadron ends just like the T-45 Goshawk with the Carrier Qualifications. Here again the pilot will first fly the FLCP reconstructed on a flight deck on a normal runway. Although it is never the reality of a floating, rolling and pounding aircraft carrier at sea, it is the only thing that comes close to simulate a landing at an aircraft carrier. The FLCP are initially flown with an instructor pilot in the back but the first real landing on a real carrier at sea is always flown solo, Sqn Com. Flea joked, "Would you like to sit in the backseat as an instructor during an initial approach of a pilot in training?!".

Carrier Cruise

After completion of the FRS, the pilot is assigned in a traditional ceremony to an operational squadron on an aircraft carrier. Every 3 months a new pilot flows in from the FRS into a squadron. This phased flow gives the other pilots of the squadron the opportunity to have enough time and atten-

Superhornet attached to the flightdeck just before sunset

Bolter! This Superhornet missed all 4 arresting cables during landing and is forced to re-launch with tailhook down

tion to further training and coaching of the new pilot. Almost daily the pilot flies together with experienced colleagues to train on the use of the F(A)-18 as a weapon platform. Often with nothing but open sea around the ship, there are plenty of opportunities for training radar interceptions and low-level strike missions.

During an operational cruise of over 6 months, there is little room for family, friends or hobbies and this makes the learning curve on board at the ship very high. During the visit of the authors the USS Dwight D. Eisenhower operated near the coast of Pakistan to support ground troops in Afghanistan. After only a few months a new pilot is able to fly as wingman on these operational war missions. It is no exception that real combat operations are performed during these flights. Sqn. Com Flea explains, "It is precisely this kind of real missions which makes a rookie pilot a mature fighter pilot in a short time".

The conditions on board of the aircraft carrier are often not easily and precisely in this demanding strange environment it is expected from the brand new pilot to show what qualities he is made of. The pilots of a squadron of fighter planes are normally already a close group and it will surprise no one that the bands on board of the ship will be even closer. "Within the squadron there is a healthy competition between the pilots with no evening or weekend to escape. That is not always easy for a rookie who is expected to prove his skills to his experienced colleagues 7 days per week. It is very important to find a responsible way to deal with this situation." Sqn Com. Flea concludes, "Working and living in this area is one of the unusual aspects which makes flying from an aircraft carrier so special for the pilots."

Photos by Frank van der Avoort and Johan Franken

After returning from a mission over Afganistan the pilot walks on the flightdeck

A hornet crew fully dressed walks towards the debriefing room

16051
SUPER DRAWINGS IN 3D
Dmitry Mironov
The Japanese Battleship
Nagato
KAGERO
Buy now on shop.kagero.pl
shop.kagero.pl • shop.kagero.pl

16052
SUPER DRAWINGS IN 3D
Carlo Cestra
The Italian Heavy Cruiser
Pola
KAGERO
Coming Soon

The Italian Heavy Cruiser Pola

The Italian Heavy Cruiser Pola, 1941

3D Anaglyph
Carlo Cestra

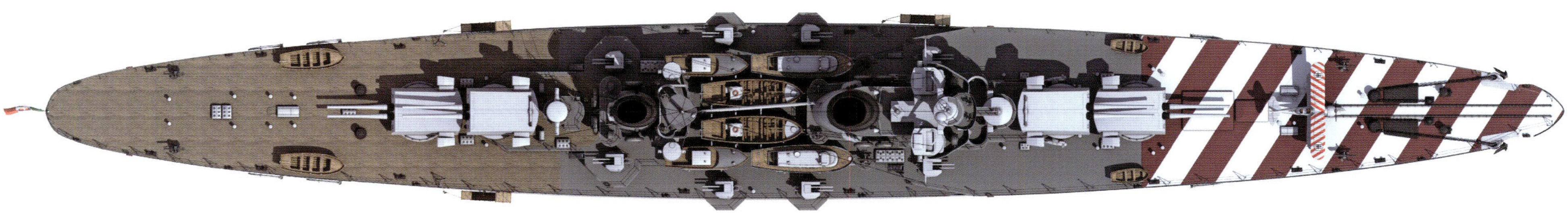

POLA

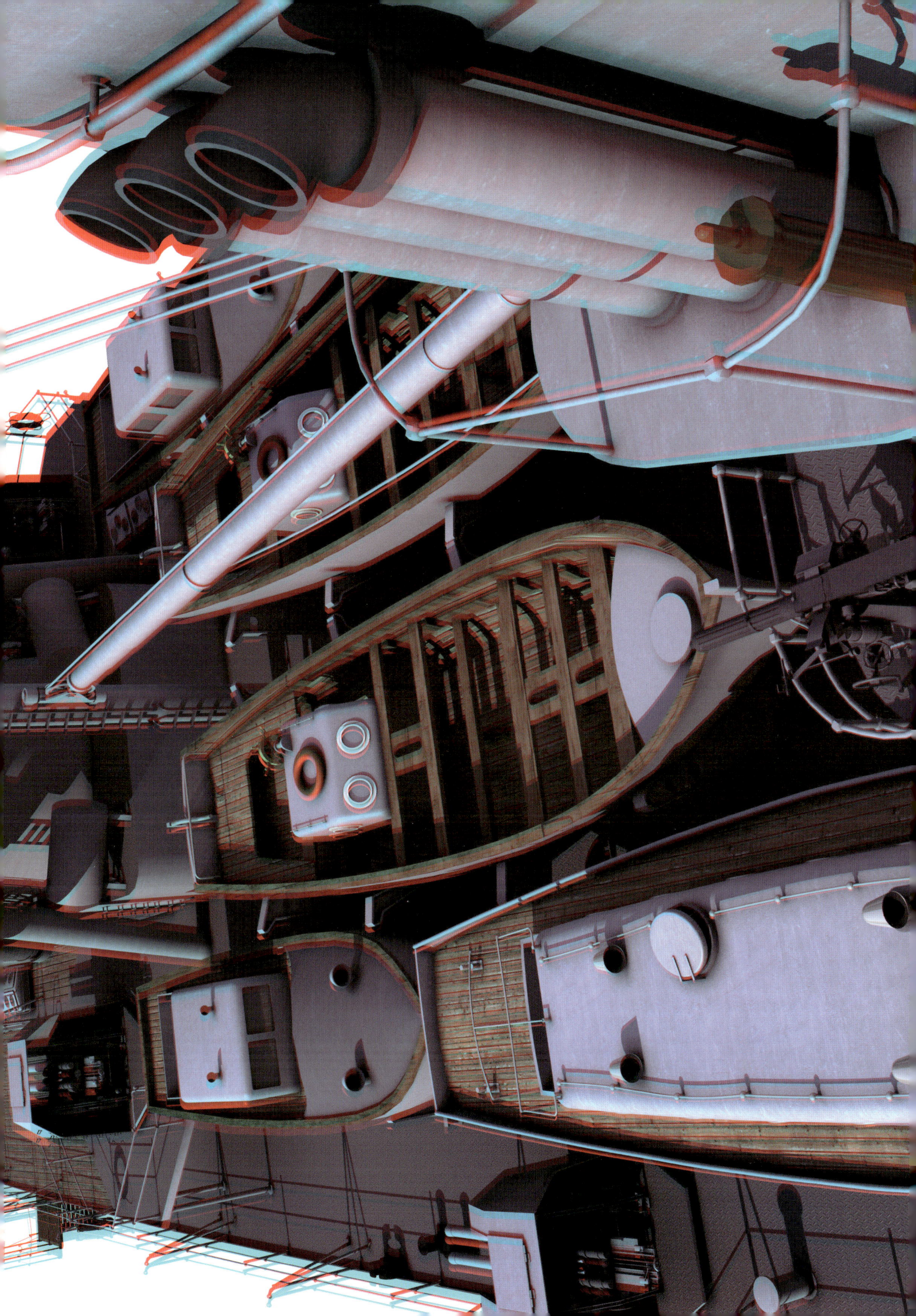

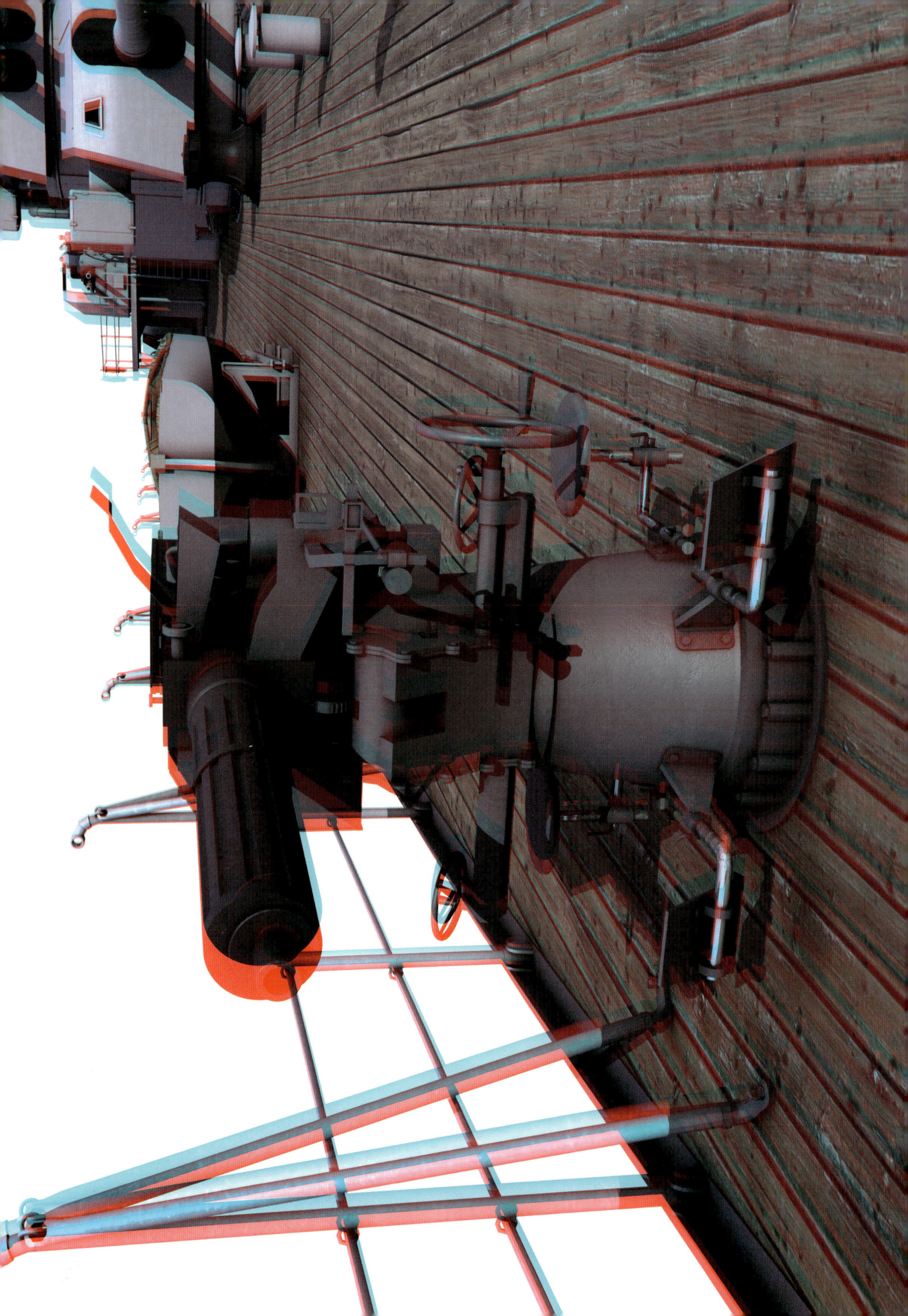